A Child's Introduction to
THE WORLD

A Child's Introduction to
THE WORLD

Geography, Cultures and People—
From the Grand Canyon to the Great Wall of China

By Heather Alexander • Illustrated by Meredith Hamilton

BLACK DOG
& LEVENTHAL
PUBLISHERS
NEW YORK

A Child's Introduction to the World: Geography, Cultures, and People —
From the Grand Canyon to the Great Wall of China

Copyright ©2010 by Black Dog & Leventhal Publishers, Inc.
Original artwork copyright ©2010 by Meredith Hamilton

Published by
Black Dog & Leventhal Publishers, Inc.
151 West 19th Street
New York, NY 10011

Distributed by
Workman Publishing Company
225 Varick Street
New York, NY 10014

Manufactured in China

Cover and interior design by Sheila Hart Design

ISBN-13: 978-1-57912-832-6

Library of Congress Cataloging-in-Publication Data available on file.
h g f e d c b a

To Liv, Phee, and "Joe"—you are my world.

H. A.

For all the places I have been lucky enough to live in:
Austin, Texas; Brooklyn, New York; Cushing's Island, Maine;
Paris, France; and Singapore.

M. H.

Contents

Part One: Where Am I?

Part Two: Welcome to the World

Part 1
WHERE AM I?

Picture this: You wake up one morning, and you are in a strange, new land. You have no idea how you got there or why (play along—okay?). There are no people. There are no buildings. You don't recognize anything.

"WHERE am I?" you shriek.

You don't have a cell phone—you're totally on your own. Now what? You're going have to use the world around you for clues. You decide walk around. Are there hills and valleys, or is the land very flat? You notice where certain trees and plants grow. You check out the animals that are scurrying about. You make note of the weather and temperature. Is there water nearby? Is it salty or fresh? You search out a freshwater stream, then mark the path—you'll need to find the water again. You grab a stick and scratch all you have learned about this new land in the dirt, so you'll remember it later.

Clue 1: Land

Clue 2: Climate

Clue 3: Plants

Clue 4: Animals

Okay, you're still stranded in a strange place, but now you have a better idea of your new environment. Why? You've just used **geography**!

Most kids think geography is just memorizing where countries are and the names of their capitals. It's *so* much more. The word "geography" comes from the Greek language. "Geo" means Earth, and "graphy" means "to write or describe," so "geography" means "to describe the Earth." In fact, some people have said that geography tries to make sense of everything that happens on the surface of the Earth. Whew! That's a huge topic! But, no worries, we're going to break it down.

Basically, geography is anything that can be put on a map—the Earth's surface, the people and animals that live there, the weather and climate, and all the rocks, minerals, plants, landforms, and oceans.

Most geographers—people who study geography—try to answer three questions:

1. **Where?**
2. **Why there?**
3. **Why do we care?**

In this book, we'll discover the answers. We'll explore the world together, from the largest oceans to driest desert to the smallest country. We'll learn how maps are made, and we'll tackle how to read them. We'll figure out where you are right this very minute and open your eyes to fabulous places you may wish to visit in the future. We'll discover how the Earth affects you, *and* how you affect the Earth.

The world, though, is not just about places. It is about people, too. Our world is made up of many kinds of people and many different cultures, each with its own customs and traditions. What may seem "normal" to you may be strange to a child halfway across the world—and the other way around. Learning about the culture of a country—its holidays, festivals, foods, languages, and way of life—is the best way to understand that country and its people.

But there's one thing we're *not* going to do. We're not going to lecture you or bore you with things you can't understand. Geography and learning about the world is fun. It is all about the land you stand on, the country you live in, the stories you've read, and the faraway places you've see on TV. Plus, check out the inside cover of the book for a cool paper globe!

Abbreviations to Know

SOMETIMES WE DON'T HAVE THE SPACE TO WRITE OUT THE WHOLE WORD, SO WE TAKE A SHORT CUT. HERE ARE THE ONES TO LOOK FOR:

FT=FEET

IN=INCHES

MI=MILES

M= METERS

CM=CENTIMETERS

KM= KILOMETERS

°=DEGREES

F=FAHRENHEIT

C=CELCIUS

%=PERCENT

Let's begin at the beginning—the formation of Earth. Scientists found some very, very old rocks, measured their age, and estimated that Earth is about 4.6 billion years old. That number looks like:

4,600,000,000

That's old! To give you a better idea of exactly how old: Dinosaurs roamed the Earth about 230 million (230,000,000) years ago. Humans appeared about 100,000 years ago. The first airplane was invented a little more than 100 years ago.

Third Rock from the Sun

Earth is a small planet in an enormous **universe**, which means *everything* that exists *everywhere*! Our part of the universe is called the **solar system**. There are eight planets in the solar system and they all orbit, or circle, an enormous mega-hot star that we call the Sun. Earth is the third planet from the Sun and the fifth largest planet in our solar system.

The solar system and about 100 billion stars make up our **galaxy**, which is called the **Milky Way**. People say it was named the Milky Way because if you stare at the sky on a clear night, all the stars together look like a puddle of spilled milk. A lot of other galaxies (we have no idea how many) are way, way out there as well, and together they all form the universe.

There's No Place like Home...

Earth is the only planet (at least, the only planet we know of) where people, animals, and plants can survive. That's because Earth has oxygen in its **atmosphere**. Think of atmosphere as a blanket of air that surrounds the Earth. It protects all living things on the Earth from the intense heat of the Sun and flying objects from outer space—it's like pulling the covers over your head in bed to stay safe and cozy.

Why Is Earth Called the Blue Planet?

Look at a photo of Earth from outer space, and you'll see mostly blue, with a little bit of green. What's all that blue? Water, of course. Seventy-one percent of Earth is covered by water. Earth has so much water is should really be called the Water Planet! The little bit of green is land that is divided into seven **continents**, or huge chunks of land.

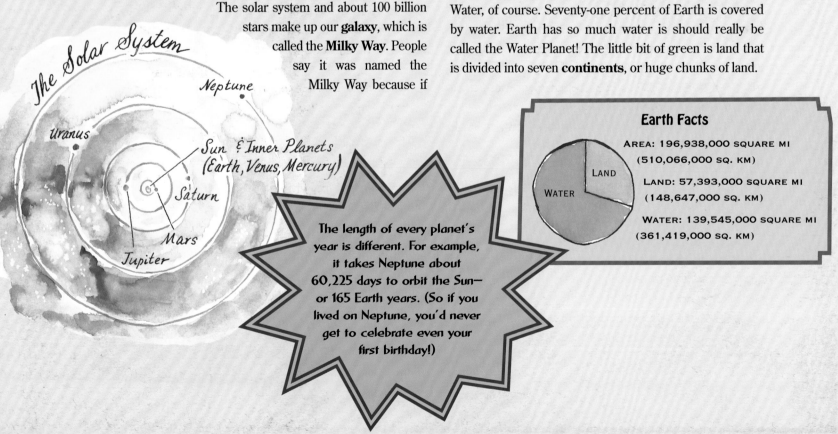

The Solar System

Neptune

Uranus

Sun & Inner Planets
(Earth, Venus, Mercury)

Saturn

Mars

Jupiter

The length of every planet's year is different. For example, it takes Neptune about 60,225 days to orbit the Sun— or 165 Earth years. (So if you lived on Neptune, you'd never get to celebrate even your first birthday!)

Earth Facts

WATER | LAND

AREA: 196,938,000 SQUARE MI (510,066,000 SQ. KM)

LAND: 57,393,000 SQUARE MI (148,647,000 SQ. KM)

WATER: 139,545,000 SQUARE MI (361,419,000 SQ. KM)

The Milky Way Galaxy

Our solar system

Going Round and Round

On Earth, we're always moving in circles. Earth's journey around the Sun is 590 million miles (950 million km). One time around takes 365.25 days, and this amount of time is known as a **year**. But what happens to that extra ¼ (0.25) of a day left over each year? If we ignore it, all the extra parts of a day will start to pile up and after a while, the seasons would fall in the wrong months. A smart guy named **Julius Caesar** decided to add an extra day to our calendar every four years. The extra day is added on February 29, because many years ago, the calendar ended the year with February—so that was the natural place to tack on an extra day. The years with the extra day are called **leap years** and the extra day (February 29) is called Leap Day.

Night and Day

At the same time we rotate around the Sun, our planet is also spinning on its own **axis**. The axis is an imaginary line through the center of Earth. Earth makes one full spin on its axis every twenty-four hours, moving us from day to night and back into day. Light from the Sun shines on Earth as it spins, but it only lights up half of our planet at one time. Most people get about twelve hours of light and twelve hours of darkness every day. This gives us time to go to school or work and to play, and it also gives our bodies time to rest and sleep.

Day

Night

MATH ATTACK

¼ + ¼ + ¼ + ¼ = ⁴⁄₄ = 1 day

Earth Time

ONE ROTATION
ON AXIS = 1 DAY

ONE ROTATION
AROUND SUN
= 1 YEAR

250

Years Ago (in millions)

125

0
(now)

Excuse Me, I Think We're Floating!

Now you know Earth is always spinning, but did you know that all the land and oceans are moving, too?

Take a look at the paper globe from the inside cover of this book. Now pretend you are doing a puzzle. Do you see the continents that could fit together? What about South America sliding next to southern Africa? And North America interlocking with northern Africa?

Scientists believe that 250 million years ago, there weren't separate continents—the Earth had just one big land mass surrounded by water. A German **geologist** (that's a person who studies the history of the Earth, using rocks) named Alfred Wegener called this supercontinent a **pangaea**, which means "all the land" in Greek. Pangaea was C-shaped, and its land ran from one end of the Earth to the other. (That means that dinosaurs could have wandered from the South Pole up to the North Pole—and back!)

Here's Why Everything Moved...

The Earth is made up of three layers: the **core**, the **mantle**, and the **crust**.

The Earth's crust isn't solid. It is cracked into about twenty huge slabs called **tectonic plates**. They act like huge rafts and float on the liquid of the mantle. The tremendous heat and pressure of the mantle's liquid causes the plates to move constantly in all directions. This is called **continental drift**. Over the last 220 million years, the plates have shifted and floated to where they are now.

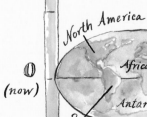

- THE CRUST IS THE OUTER, AND THINNEST, LAYER. IT IS MADE UP OF SOIL AND ROCKS. THE LAND WE WALK ON AND THE LAND UNDER THE OCEANS ARE PART OF THE CRUST.

- THE MANTLE IS THE MIDDLE LAYER. IT IS COMPOSED OF SUPER-HOT LIQUID ROCK, CALLED **MAGMA**.

- THE CORE, WHICH IS IN THE CENTER, HAS TWO PARTS: THE OUTER CORE AND THE INNER CORE. THE OUTER CORE IS MADE UP OF LIQUID IRON. THE INNER CORE IS SOLID IRON, AND IT IS THE HOTTEST PART OF THE EARTH. ITS TEMPERATURE IS ALMOST AS HOT AS THE SUN.

How Do the Plates Know Where to Go?

They don't. Sometimes, plates rub or bump each other as they pass. This causes earthquakes and volcanoes. Sometimes, plates ram into each other in a head-on collision, and mountains rise up because the edges of the plates overlap. For example, India was once a separate landmass. About 120 million years ago, it began to move north, and slowly it joined up with Asia. Actually, it probably bumped into Asia pretty hard, because when it did, it created the Himalaya Mountains.

Are We Really Still Moving?

Yep. Drifting, actually. The Earth's plates move only about ½ to 4 inches a year (1 to 10 cm). You don't feel it because that's slower than your fingernails grow. Every year India scoots a little more northward, and every year the Himalayas grow about 1 inch (2.5 cm) higher! Geologists believe that the Atlantic Ocean is widening and that North America is moving farther away from Europe and Africa. They also say Australia is heading north and will collide with Asia. But if you live down under, don't take out your crash helmets just yet. It will probably take another 100 million years to get there. And some geologists are predicting that in 220 million years, we may all come back together in a new pangaea. It really will be a small world after all then—won't it?

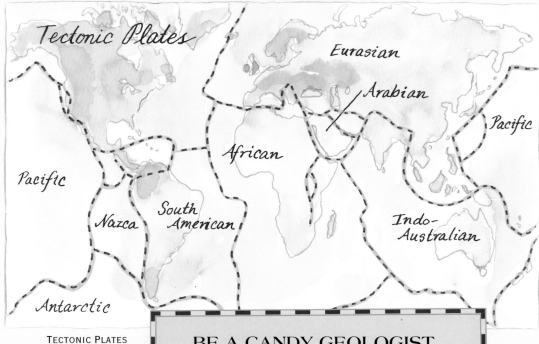

TECTONIC PLATES
OF THE WORLD

BE A CANDY GEOLOGIST

Use a candy bar to see
how plate tectonics works.

1. First, wash your hands. Then place a Milky Way® or Snickers® candy bar on a paper napkin. Do you know which parts of the candy bar represent which layers of the Earth?

   - The chocolate on the top represents the crust of the Earth.
   - The caramel layer represents the mantle.
   - The light brown layer (nougat) represents the outer core.
   - The bottom layer of chocolate is the inner core.

2. Using your fingernail, make a few breaks in the chocolate "crust" of the candy bar. These are the plates.

3. Gently hold the candy bar at both ends. Pull the candy apart. Now push it from side to side. Then move it back together. Did you see how the plates collided, bumped, and separated? This is what happens to the Earth with plate tectonics.

4. Don't forget to eat the Earth—yum!

Pretend you lived thousands of years ago. Things were very different back then. No TVs. No computers. No cars. You lived in a tiny village and never traveled farther than you could walk. When you looked down your village's main dirt path everything looked flat, so you probably believed the Earth was flat, too.

Newsflash! It's not.

So how did people figure out the truth?

The world is as flat as a GRAPE LEAF...

First Came Aristotle...

Aristotle (AH-riss-tot-ul) was a Greek philosopher (a philosopher tries to find answers to tough questions about life) who lived in the fourth century BC. While he was studying the Moon, there was a **lunar eclipse**. A lunar eclipse is when Earth moves between the Sun and the Moon, blocking the Sun's light to the Moon. The shadow of Earth that he saw on the Moon was round. Now, Aristotle was a smart dude, so he knew that only a round object can cast a round shadow.

Therefore...Earth was round, not flat.

But Didn't Christopher Columbus Prove the World Wasn't Flat?

Yes—and no. Aristotle and his smart Greek friends knew the world was round thousands of years before Columbus did. Claudius Ptolemy (TAHL-uh-mee) drew the first map of the world in 150 AD, and he wrote a famous book about Earth being a **sphere**, which means round. Then lots of people said Aristotle and Ptolemy were wrong. They convinced other folks, and soon Aristotle and Ptolemy's maps and books were thrown away or hidden. After hundreds of years, people forgot about those smart Greek guys and believed—*again*—that the world was flat.

Hear me well... The Earth is flat. You could fall off if you are not careful.

ARISTOTLE

Enter Christopher Columbus. In 1479, he was a mapmaker on a little island off the coast of Portugal. He'd found Ptolemy's maps and heard stories of a round world. He also heard from travelers about the riches in the Indies (Asia). Until then, Europeans had to take a long, hard journey across mountains and deserts called the Silk Road to reach Asia. Columbus was sure he could reach the

Indies faster by sailing a ship westward, across the ocean. He convinced the king and queen of Spain to give him supplies, three ships (the *Niña*, the *Pinta*, and the *Santa Maria*), and a crew of eighty-eight men for a journey of exploration. His goal wasn't to prove the world was round (he *knew* that already). It was to find a faster route to get to all the good loot. He set sail on August 3, 1492.

On October 12, 1492, Columbus and his crew landed on an island eventually named San Salvador. He was 100% sure he was in the Indies. But he wasn't—not even close. He had just "discovered" the New World, soon to be called North America.

So What Went Wrong?

Columbus used Ptolemy's maps, which showed the **circumference**—the distance all the way around the Earth—to be 7,000 miles (11,000 km) smaller than we know it really is. Poor Columbus—he thought Asia was a lot closer. Also, Columbus had no idea there was a huge mass of land (North America and South America) blocking his path.

About 40 million people were living on North America and South America when Columbus docked. Columbus said he discovered a new land. But how can you really "find" something that millions of people already know about?

Magellan Seals the Deal

Aristotle proved the world was round. So did Ptolemy and Columbus. But **Ferdinand Magellan** (ma-JELL-an) made a voyage that ended all the flat-or-not debates forever.

Magellan was a Portuguese explorer who sailed westward from Spain in 1519 to reach the East Indies, just as Columbus had tried. Magellan and his crew of two hundred and fifty men rounded the tip of South America and went into the Pacific Ocean. And he kept on going. In 1521, he landed in the Philippines, where the natives flung poison arrows at him and killed him. His crew sailed on without him, and in 1522, three years after they had left Spain, eighteen crew members returned to it. This was the first voyage around the world, showing everyone that Earth really was round.

Columbus' Route

The Silk Road

Magellan's Route

I wanted to go around the globe, but I thought it was SMALLER and I didn't make it...

My crew went around the globe, but I DIED en route.

Christopher Columbus

Ferdinand Magellan

Once all the explorers and scientists agreed that Earth was round, they needed a system to figure out exactly where places were located.

Looking for Some Direction

Direction is the way you are facing. There are four main directions: north, east, south, and west. These are called **cardinal directions**. They are written using initials: N, E, S, W.

If you are facing toward north, south will be behind you, west will be on your left, and east will be on your right.

Here's a funny way to remember the order of cardinal directions: **N**ever **E**at **S**quirmy **W**orms.

Getting Back to Earth

Pretend you are holding one of those bouncy, red playground balls, and pretend it's the Earth. You want to find out where you are and how far it is to a cool, new place you want to visit. But wait, a ball has no corners or edges. So what do you use as a point to make a measurement? Think back. Remember the imaginary axis that the Earth spins on? The ends of the axis are called the **North Pole** and the **South Pole** (the top and bottom of your ball), and the two poles can be used as measuring points.

Now picture an imaginary line that circles the exact middle of the ball, or the Earth. This line is called the **equator**. The equator divides the Earth into two equal halves. The half above the equator is called the **northern hemisphere** and the half below the equator is called the **southern hemisphere**. The word "hemisphere" means half of a ball (in this case, the Earth). What hemisphere do you live in?

Quick—Where Do You Live?

You probably answered with a street address or the name of a town. But what if all the signs were taken down? What if you had to tell someone who lived on the other side of the world where your house is located, and you didn't have an address to give?

That's what **latitude** and **longitude** are all about. Latitude and longitude are horizontal and vertical lines that intersect to create a **grid**. Every spot on Earth—no matter if it is in the middle of a desert or in an ocean—can be found on this global grid if you have two special numbers, or **coordinates**.

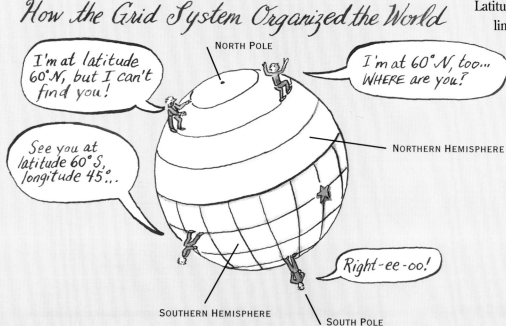

How the Grid System Organized the World

I'm at latitude 60°N, but I can't find you!

I'm at 60°N, too... WHERE are you?

See you at latitude 60°S, longitude 45°...

Right-ee-oo!

NORTH POLE

NORTHERN HEMISPHERE

SOUTHERN HEMISPHERE

SOUTH POLE

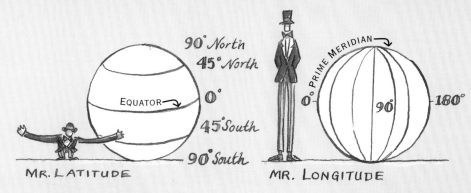

MR. LATITUDE

MR. LONGITUDE

I've Got Latitude Attitude!

Let's use our paper globe again. Pretend someone has drawn lots of lines that are equal distances apart, above and below the equator. These are called lines of **latitude** (or **parallels**). Latitude measures how far north or south a place is from the equator. Latitude is measured in degrees: ninety degrees north of the equator, and ninety degrees south of the it.

The equator is 0° latitude.
The North Pole is 90°N latitude.
The South Pole is 90°S latitude.

Now let's say someone tells you there is buried treasure at 10°N. You want to dig it up, so you find the equator and count ten lines (or degrees) up to the north. But wait—the latitude line runs all the way around the Earth. The town could be *anywhere* on that line. So after you find the treasure's north/south position (latitude), you need to find its east/west position. How do you do that?

You Need Longitude

Longitude lines run up and down from the North Pole to the South Pole (picture the way the lines go on a pumpkin). Longitude lines are also called **meridians**. Meridians always cross the equator, but meridians are not equal distances apart. Longitude measures how far east or west a place is from an imaginary longitude line called the **prime meridian**, which is in Greenwich, England. This town was chosen as the longitude starting point because a famous astronomy observatory used to be there.

Longitude is measured using 360° because a sphere measures 360° around its circumference.

Back to the Buried Treasure

The treasure has the coordinates 10°N and 30°W. You already found 10°N (that's the latitude). Now look for the prime meridian and move 30° to the west (that's the longitude). The point where the latitude and longitude lines cross is where the treasure is. (You should be pointing to a spot deep in the ocean. Time to rent a boat—or a submarine—for your treasure hunt!)

MATH ATTACK 180° + 180° = 360°

Coordinates for Cool Places

MOUNT EVEREST
27°N 86°E

GRAND CANYON
36°N 112°W

GREAT BARRIER REEF
18°S 146°E

TAJ MAHAL
27°N 78°E

EIFFEL TOWER
48°N 2°E

Living on a Line

CAN YOU FIND ALL EIGHT COUNTRIES THAT ARE ON THE PRIME MERIDIAN? THEY ARE: *UNITED KINGDOM, FRANCE, SPAIN, ALGERIA, MALI, BURKINA FASO, GHANA,* AND *TOGO.*

HOW ABOUT THE ELEVEN COUNTRIES THAT LIE ON THE EQUATOR? THEY ARE: *BRAZIL, COLUMBIA, ECUADOR, INDONESIA, SOMALIA, KENYA, UGANDA, DEMOCRATIC REPUBLIC OF THE CONGO, REPUBLIC OF THE CONGO, GABON,* AND *TOME AND PRINCIPE.*

When Are We?

How do you measure time? Some people measure it in minutes, some people measure it in days, some by seasons, and some by years. Before there were clocks and calendars, people used the Sun to track the passing of time.

What Time Is It?

Noon is when the Sun is at the highest point in the sky. So is it noon at the same time all over the world? No—the Earth is always rotating, so the Sun cannot be at its highest point over Los Angeles and Paris at the same time.

In 1884, the world decided to create an international time-telling system. Before then, you pretty much looked at the sky, saw where the Sun was, and then guessed the time. If it was really 5:30 p.m. and you thought it was 6:00 p.m., it was no big deal—so what if you ate dinner a little early? Then came railroads and the telegraph, and suddenly time mattered. With people guessing the time (and not doing such a great job of it), trains smashed into each other on railroad tracks.

So world leaders and scientists had a meeting in Washington DC. They divided the world into twenty-four parts. Each part was one hour (this equaled the twenty-four hours in a day). The sections were called **time zones**, and they were 15° longitude apart because the Earth spins 15° every hour.

MATH ATTACK $360° \div 24 = 15°$

Time zones have to do with the position of the Sun on the Earth's surface. When it's noon in Boston, it is also noon in Bogotá, Colombia, even though Bogotá is so much farther south. This is because both cities are in the same unit of longitude. This doesn't work for latitude. Los Angeles and New York have almost the same latitude, but when it is 5:00 p.m. in New York, it is only 2:00 p.m. in Los Angeles. Why? Because Los Angeles is three time zones—or 45° of longitude—away from New York.

MATH ATTACK $15° \times 3 = 45°$

Los Angeles, USA
10 o'clock p.m. Sunday

London, England
6 o'clock a.m. Monday

Moscow, Russia
9 o'clock a.m. Monday

Hanoi, Vietnam
2 o'clock p.m. Monday

New York, USA
1 o'clock a.m. Monday

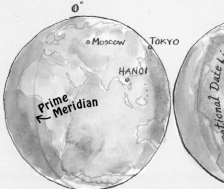

Tokyo, Japan
3 o'clock p.m. Monday

West ←——————————→ East

How Can Today Be Monday if Yesterday Was Monday?

Good question. Let's say you are going on a trip around the world, heading east. You cross one time zone, then another, then another until you get back to the place where you started. What do you do now? Start the same day again? Imagine repeating the same day at school over and over—scary!

People didn't know where one day ended and the next one started. So the people at this big meeting created the **international date line** (IDL) at the 180° meridian, directly across from the prime meridian (0°). The IDL is used to mark the start of a new twenty-hour-hour day—it is where Sunday becomes Monday.

- **If you are standing on the IDL and you travel west, you move ahead one day.**
- **If you travel east, you move back one day.**
- **If you put one foot on each side of the line, you can be in two days at the same time!**

The IDL runs through the Pacific Ocean, zigzagging around the islands of Fiji so that country will not be split into two days.

The Four Seasons

Did you know that kids in Australia celebrate Christmas during their summertime? Yep, on the night of December 24, Santa has to leave his red jacket in the sleigh and wriggle into some swimming trunks when he delivers gifts to the Southern Hemisphere. Just as time is different for everyone around the world, the seasons are different, too.

In the Northern Hemisphere, summer is June, July, and August.

In the Southern Hemisphere, summer is December, January, and February.

A Crooked Earth Gives Us Seasons

Earth's always leaning to one side, because it is tilted on its axis. This tilt of about 23° makes the seasons change as Earth orbits around the Sun. Here's how it works: The amount of heat the Sun gives off is always the same. If the Sun shines from overhead directly on a place, that place gets very hot (hot = summer). But if the Sun shines on that place at an angle, the heat is less intense and that place is cooler (cool = winter). In June, for example, the Sun shines directly on the Northern Hemisphere because that hemisphere is pointed toward the Sun that time of year. The Southern Hemisphere gets fewer of the Sun's rays in June, so it is cold there. If Earth wasn't tilted, we'd have only one season.

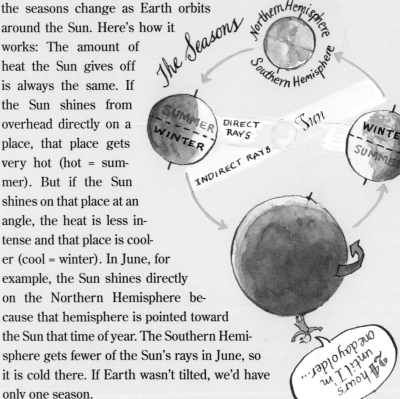

The Seasons · Northern Hemisphere · Southern Hemisphere · SUMMER WINTER · DIRECT RAYS · Sun · WINTER SUMMER · INDIRECT RAYS

24 hours until I'm one day older...

BE THE FLASHLIGHT SUN

Find a flashlight that has a bright beam (the flashlight will act as the Sun). Take it with you inside a dark room or closet. Turn on the flashlight and hold it directly above the floor or some other flat object. You should see a round, bright circle of light. Now hold the flashlight the same distance away from the floor, but hold it on an angle. Notice that the light is not as bright. Why? Because the light has a lot more distance to cover, just like when the Sun shines on Earth at an angle.

Map Stories

aps are like stories. They can tell action-filled tales about wars won or lost, lands discovered, trips taken or planned, even where diseases' spread.

The first maps, made by cavemen (and cavewomen!), were scratched into the dirt, using sticks and stones. Symbols were used for trees, mountains, or other landmarks. But what happened if it rained and the map washed away? Or if you walked halfway there and couldn't remember if you should turn left or right by the wooly mammoth?

Soon people figured out how to use different materials to make maps they could take with them. Over time, maps have been sketched on soft clay that was hardened by the sun, carved into stone tablets, drawn with berry juice on animal hides, painted on silk, woven into reeds, printed on paper, and stored on computers. The word "map" comes from the Latin word mappa, which means "cloth."

After agreeing that maps were way better than following a trail of bread crumbs back home, people got really into making maps, or **cartography**. People who make maps are called cartographers. They can show almost anything on a map—from the amount of rainfall throughout the world to the location of volcanoes to where chocolate ice cream is the most popular. Some of the most common kinds of maps are:

Physical Map

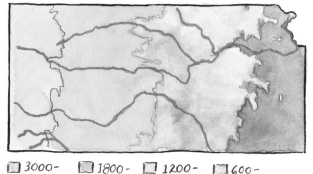

Feet Above Sea Level

3000-4500 | 1800-3000 | 1200-1800 | 600-1200

- A PHYSICAL MAP, WHICH SHOWS LANDFORMS AND BODIES OF WATER—BASICALLY THE NATURAL WORLD AROUND YOU. ONE TYPE OF PHYSICAL MAP IS A RELIEF MAP, ALSO KNOWN AS A TOPOGRAPHICAL MAP, WHICH IS BUMPY TO SHOW HOW HIGH OR LOW THE LAND IS.

Political Map

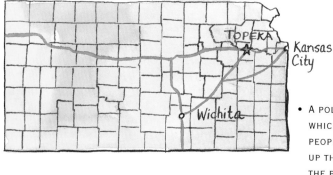

Counties, Major Cities and Highways

TOPEKA
Kansas City
Wichita

- A POLITICAL MAP, WHICH SHOWS HOW PEOPLE HAVE DIVIDED UP THE WORLD AND THE BOUNDARIES THEY HAVE CREATED.

Thematic Map

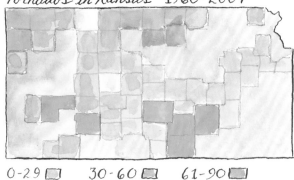

Tornados in Kansas 1960-2007

0-29 | 30-60 | 61-90

- A THEMATIC MAP, WHICH SHOWS SPECIFIC INFO, SUCH AS WEATHER, POPULATION, RELIGIONS, OR LANGUAGES.

How to Read a Map

You have front-row tickets to a cool concert at a place you've never been before. You have three choices: (1) wander the streets and hope you luckily bump into a line of screaming fans, (2) ask someone for directions (and cross your fingers they're right), or (3) read a map. If you want to be sure to see the concert, reading a map is your best bet. Here's how:

Symbols are the secret codes of maps. They are simple drawings that show what and where things are. Symbols are used because there is no room on a map to draw a lot of pictures.

The **key** is the list on the side of the map that tells you what the symbols mean. The key is also called the **legend**, because it tells the story of the map.

Maps are smaller than the area they show. You can tell the distance from one place to another because maps are drawn to **scale**. A good example of scale is if you built a dollhouse version of your house. If your real bedroom measured 20 feet across, and your scale was 1 inch = 5 feet, then you would build a bedroom in your dollhouse that was 4 in across. Scale is either shown as a scale bar or written as a ratio or a fraction. The numerator (usually 1) represents the distance on the map. The denominator (the big number) shows the distance on Earth.

Guess The Symbols

A. B. C. D. E. F. G.

(answers below)

THE GUIDE to Map Symbols

1:1 or $\frac{1}{1}$ *Real World* (Bedroom = 15 feet long)

1:10 or $\frac{1}{10}$ *Doll House* (1 inch = 10 feet)

1:30 or $\frac{1}{30}$ *Mouse's Doll House* (1 inch = 30 feet)

MATH ATTACK $20 \div 5 = 4$

A. Theme park B. Parking C. Bathroom D. Bank E. Post Office F. Forest G. Hospital

On a map you will also find a **compass rose**. It's not really a flower, although long ago it was drawn with many points so it looked like one. It shows the four cardinal directions. If you know the cardinal directions, they you can find the **intermediate direction**, which is the direction between the cardinal directions. The intermediate direction between south and west is southwest, or SW—get it?

Most maps are made with the north on the top and the south at the bottom. But there's no real reason the north should be at the top. Take a world map and turn it upside down. It's still correct, but doesn't it look funny?

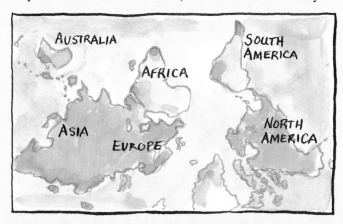

Hello, Down There!

A map usually shows an area from above. This is called bird's-eye view—as if you were a bird flying in the sky and looking down. In the 1700s and 1800s, mapmakers went up in hot air balloon to better see the rivers, mountains, and coastlines. In the 1900s, they went up in airplanes. Starting in 1950, mapmakers began to use cameras and aerial photography became very important to cartography. (**Aerial** means up in the air.)

In the late 1950s, satellites were sent hundreds of miles into outer space, and they took photos that showed incredible details of Earth. Satellite photos are awesome for mapping hard-to-reach places like rainforests or the Arctic.

The Talking Map

Is there a talking map in your parents' car? That's called a **GPS** (Global Positioning System) receiver, and it makes finding places super easy! Over twenty-seven GPS satellites are orbiting way above Earth. Each satellite has its own path, and as it circles our planet, it sends a radio signal back down to Earth. But this isn't the kind of radio that plays music—the signal is more like a buzzing noise. Your GPS receiver picks up the signal from at least four different satellites, then it analyzes exactly where you are at that very moment, and tells you where to go next.

LOST? BLAME THE COMPUTER!

Your family is about to go on a big car trip to visit relatives. Years ago, Mom or Dad would open a huge map on the kitchen table and use a pen to mark their driving route. But today, they probably go online and the computer automatically prints out directions. How does the computer know how to get to your Aunt Melissa's house? First, the computer converts the starting and ending points into latitude and longitude coordinates. This is called geocoding. Then it looks at all the possible driving routes from your house to your aunt's house. It picks the fastest, most direct route, based on the kinds of roads, how fast a car is allowed to drive on those roads, and the number of curves and stoplights on the roads. Pretty amazing, huh?

GPS is our co-pilot...

MAP IT!

Let's pretend there's a new kid in your class at school, and you invite him to play at your house after school. But your mom picks you up early that day to go to the dentist. The new kid is going to have to walk from school to your house all by himself, and he doesn't know the way. How will he get there? You have an idea—you'll draw him a map. Let's give it a try.

1. Take a plain piece of paper. Now pretend you are flying in a plane and looking down at your neighborhood. What would you see? In the middle of the page, draw what is at the center of your neighborhood.

2. Next, draw your house and then your school. Think about where they are in relation to each other and in relation to the center of the neighborhood. Use a ruler to help draw all the roads between the two places.

3. Think about landmarks between your school and your house. Is there a post office, a bank, a store, a park, or a fire station nearby? Draw them on your map, using symbols.

4. Add physical boundaries, such as streams, trees, and fields, and man-made boundaries, such as railroad tracks or highways.

5. Make a legend at the bottom of your map to explain what your symbols mean. Draw a compass rose showing the four cardinal directions.

6. Hopefully, your map will lead the new kid right to your front door!

23

The Ups and Downs

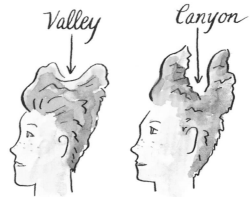

Valley   *Canyon*

Land makes up less than one-third of our planet, yet when we study the Earth, we spend a lot of time studying the land. Why? The simple answer is we live on land. Also, the land is pretty spectacular. Nature has given our planet amazing landforms—tall mountains, low valleys, deep canyons, and enormous glaciers.

Way up High

Let's start at the top. A **mountain** is land that rises more than 1,000 ft (300 m) above the surrounding land. Mountains and **mountain ranges** are found all over the world. Mount Everest in the Himalayas, in Asia, is the tallest mountain in the world—it's about 5.5 miles (8.8 km) high, the height of twenty Empire State Buildings stacked on top of one another. Mountains often reach so high into the clouds that even if the temperature is warm at the **base**, or bottom, the **peaks**, or tops, are covered in snow.

A **hill** and a **plateau** are other landforms that rise above the land around them. The differences have to do with the shape of the top. A mountain is jagged, a hill is rounded, and a plateau is flat. Think of it as someone getting a haircut. They can get a pointy, Mohawk hairdo, a bowl cut, or a buzzed flat top.

Down Deep

The low land between two mountains is called a **valley**. A narrow valley with very steep sides is called a **canyon** or a **gorge**. Canyons often have a river or a stream at the bottom. Valleys and canyons are formed when wind and water **erode** (wear away) the ground. The Colorado River, which created the Grand Canyon in Arizona, has been wearing away the Earth for millions of years. The Grand Canyon is over one mile (1.6 km) deep.

snow
peaks
clouds

Mountain   *Hill*   *Plateau*

Highest Mountains in Each Continent

ASIA:
MOUNT EVEREST (NEPAL),
29,035 FT (8,850 M)

SOUTH AMERICA:
MOUNT ACONCAGUA (ARGENTINA),
23,834 FT (6,960 M)

NORTH AMERICA:
MOUNT MCKINLEY (ALASKA),
20,320 FT (6,194 M)

AFRICA:
MOUNT KILIMANJARO (TANZANIA),
19,340 FT (5,895 M)

EUROPE:
EL'BRUS (RUSSIA/GEORGIA)
18,510 FT (5,642 M)

ANTARCTICA:
VINSON MASSIF,
16,066 FT (4,897 M)

AUSTRALIA:
MOUNT KOSCIUSKO (NEW SOUTH
WALES) 7,310 FT (2,228 M)

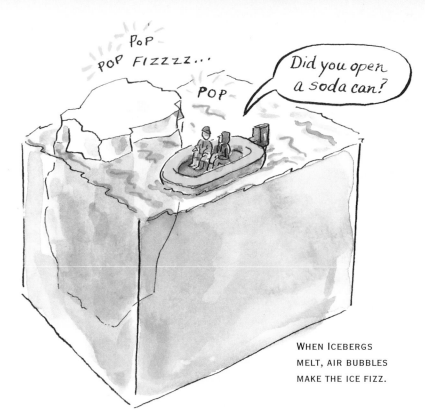

POP POP FIZZZZ...

POP

Did you open a soda can?

WHEN ICEBERGS MELT, AIR BUBBLES MAKE THE ICE FIZZ.

Ice and Snow

Several landforms are not made of dirt, rock, or sand. For example, a **glacier** is a slow-moving mass of ice. Most glaciers are found near the poles but glaciers exist on every continent. It takes thousands of years for a glacier to form. Snowfall after snowfall dumps snow in the same spot. The old snow gets pressed down really hard by the new snow and becomes solid ice, and then more new snow falls and a thick glacier forms. The weight of all that thick ice causes it to move, kind of like a slow river. When a glacier creeps out into the ocean and a piece falls off, that piece is called an **iceberg**.

Largest Glacier

LAMBERT GLACIER IN ANTARCTICA—40 MILES WIDE (64.4 KM), 320 MILES LONG (515 KM)—IS BASICALLY THE SAME LENGTH AS THE STATE OF MAINE.

Change

All landforms are constantly changing. Change is caused by erosion, weather, and people. Most of this change is so slow that we never notice it happening. Every drop of rain changes a landform in some way, often breaking away tiny pieces and moving them to other places. Strong winds and flowing water wear away at landforms, smoothing them or reshaping them. Have you ever picked up a stone from the bottom of a river and felt how smooth it was? River stones have been worn down by the force of the water. And then there's people. Cutting down trees to build houses and roads changes the land, causing the dirt to shift and move.

HEAT
WATER
WIND
HUMAN ACTIVITY

More than You See

Almost 90% of an iceberg is hidden below water. The part that you see peaking up is only 10%— or as people say, "the tip of the iceberg." Icebergs in the ocean can be dangerous, because sailors cannot see the whole thing. In 1912, a huge ship called the *Titanic* crashed into an iceberg, which tore a hole in its hull, causing it to sink. Today there is a special international patrol that watches the icebergs to make sure accidents don't happen.

Going with the Flow

What do you know about water? Okay, you know it's wet. But did you know that 80% of all living things are found in the water?

There are two kinds of water: **freshwater** (this is the stuff you can drink) and **saltwater**. Saltwater is found in the oceans and seas. The land on the Earth is divided into seven continents—but how many oceans are there?

a. **Four**

b. **One**

c. **All of the above**

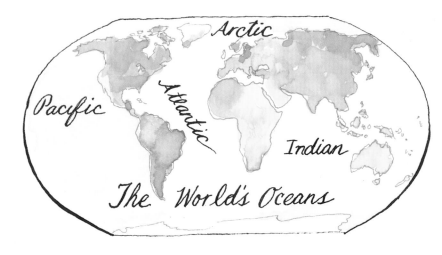

The World's Oceans

C is the correct answer. There's really just one BIG ocean flowing around the Earth, but scientists have broken it into four smaller oceans: Pacific Ocean, Atlantic Ocean, Indian Ocean, and Arctic Ocean.

Ocean Facts

ATLANTIC OCEAN
- Second-largest ocean
- Approximately 32 million sq. miles (82 million sq. km)
- Contains 20% of the world's water
- Has some of the best fishing areas, but it's also the most polluted ocean

ARCTIC OCEAN
- Smallest ocean
- Approximately 5.5 million square miles (14 million sq. km)
- Contains 4% of the world's water
- Frozen all year long

INDIAN OCEAN

- Third-largest ocean
- Approximately 28 million sq. miles (73 million sq. km)
- Contains 20% of the world's water
- Has over 5,000 islands
- 90% of this ocean is south of the equator

PACIFIC OCEAN

- Largest and deepest ocean in the world
- Approximately 70 million sq. miles (181 million sq. km)
- Contains 46% of the world's water
- Is larger than all the land on Earth put together

Saltwater Facts

SALTIEST SEA:	RED SEA
WARMEST SEA:	PERSIAN GULF
LARGEST SEA:	SOUTH CHINA SEA

Know Your Saltwater

A **SEA** IS A SMALLER OCEAN PARTIALLY SURROUNDED BY LAND.

A **BAY** IS AN AREA OF A SEA OR OCEAN MOSTLY SURROUNDED BY LAND.

A **GULF** IS LIKE A BAY, BUT BIGGER.

AN **ISLAND** IS A PIECE OF LAND, SMALLER THAN A CONTINENT, WHICH IS COMPLETELY SURROUNDED BY WATER.

AN **ARCHIPELAGO** IS A CHAIN OF ISLANDS THAT ARE CLOSE TO ONE ANOTHER. THE HAWAIIAN ISLANDS ARE AN ARCHIPELAGO.

A **PENINSULA** IS A PIECE OF LAND THAT IS SURROUNDED BY WATER ON THREE SIDES. IT OFTEN LOOKS LIKE A FINGER POINTING. THE STATE OF FLORIDA AND THE COUNTRY OF ITALY ARE PENINSULAS.

Freshwater

People and plants can live without food, but they can't live without freshwater. Did you know that *97% of the Earth's water is salty?* If all the Earth's water could fit in a gallon jug (about 3 ¾ liters) like the one milk is sold in, only one tablespoon of it would be freshwater! Saltwater can't be used for drinking or growing crops. Most of the freshwater in the world is trapped in the glaciers or is too deep underground to reach. **Only 1% of the Earth's water is usable.**

TAKING OUT THE SALT

WHEN WATER FROM THE OCEAN EVAPORATES, SALT IS LEFT OVER. THAT'S WHY THE WATER VAPOR IN THE ATMOSPHERE COMES BACK TO EARTH AS FRESHWATER RAIN. THE PROCESS OF MAKING SALTWATER DRINKABLE IS CALLED **DESALINIZATION.** NOW YOU CAN TRY IT!

1. EITHER GET 1 CUP OF SEAWATER OR MAKE YOUR OWN BY DISSOLVING 2 TEASPOONS OF SALT INTO 2 CUPS (½ LITER) OF FRESHWATER.

2. POUR THE SALTWATER INTO A LARGE, FLAT PAN.

3. BRING IT OUTSIDE INTO THE SUN OR KEEP IN A WARM, DRY PLACE.

4. WAIT.

5. WAIT SOME MORE. YOU'LL NEED TO WAIT A COUPLE OF DAYS FOR THE WATER TO EVAPORATE.

6. WHEN THE WATER IS ALL GONE, SALT SHOULD BE LEFT IN THE PAN.

Can I cook with it?

WAIT, WAIT SOME MORE...

Freshwater Facts

LONGEST RIVER:	NILE RIVER (EGYPT/ SUDAN/UGANDA)
SHORTEST RIVER:	D RIVER (OREGON, UNITED STATES)
RIVER WITH THE MOST WATER:	AMAZON RIVER (SOUTH AMERICA)
LARGEST LAKE:	CASPIAN SEA (EUROPE/ASIA)
COLDEST LAKE:	LAKE VOSTOK (ANTARCTICA)

Freshwater comes from rainwater, melting snow, and glaciers, and is found in rivers, streams, and lakes. A **river** begins high in the mountains and flows downhill until the water reaches a lake, a sea, or another large body of water. Back in the olden times, most people made their homes by a river, so they could water crops, power machines, and sail boats up- or downstream to trade. Some famous cities built on rivers are London, New York, Baghdad, Cairo, Paris, Shanghai, and Vienna.

Out of Water

The United Nations estimates that 1.1 billion people worldwide do not have clean drinking water!

All rivers do not run from north to south. They run from high ground to low ground, or the way gravity sends them.

Like Peanut Butter and Jelly

Rivers and lakes go together like peanut butter and jelly or chips and salsa. A **lake** is a body of freshwater that is surrounded by land. Rivers and lakes flow in and out of each other. Some rivers start in lakes and some end in lakes. Some lakes are so big that there are waves. A small lake that is shallow enough to grow plants on its bottom is called a **pond**.

A Flow Chart

It rains. The water not absorbed into the soil runs off into a ditch or a stream. A bunch of little streams come together and form a small river. Small rivers join together and turn into a medium-size rivers. Then a few medium-size rivers, called **tributaries,** flow into a big river. This area where rivers flow is called a **watershed**.

Streams

Small Rivers

WATERSHED

Tributary

Big Rivers

Oops! Salty Lakes

Most, but *not* every, lake is freshwater. There are some saltwater lakes: the Great Salt Lake in Utah, the Salton Sea in California, and Lake Nakuru in Kenya.

Different Spaces, Different Places

Scientists have divided the Earth into several **biomes**. A biome has its own kinds of plants and animals that live there because of the climate and the land. Biomes don't have to do with just one continent or country. They span the globe, and every biome is unique. If something in the biome changes—for example, a certain plant stops growing—this change affects every living thing in the biome. To best understand a biome, you need to know about its climate and its geography.

Climate

First off, "climate" and "weather" do not mean the same thing.

Weather means what's happening outside your window right now.

Climate is the pattern of weather in an area over a long stretch of time.

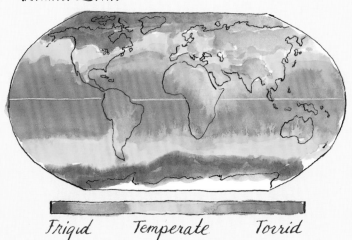

Climate Zones

Frigid   Temperate   Torrid

The amount of sunshine and rain tells you what kind of climate you're in. The Earth is divided into three **climate zones:** torrid, frigid, and temperate. The climate is hot all year long by the equator (torrid), cold all year long by the poles (frigid), and changes from hot to cold throughout the year everywhere else (temperate).

A Biome Breakdown

A **desert** is an area with very little rainfall (less than 10 inches (25 cm) of rain a year), so plants usually do not grow there. Many animals in a desert are **nocturnal**—they sleep

during the extremely hot days and move about during the cooler nights. The Sahara Desert is the world's largest desert, stretching 3.5 million sq. miles (2.2 million sq. km) across North Africa—that's almost the size of the entire United States! The world's hottest temperature, 136.4°F (58°C), was recorded in the Sahara. Not all deserts are hot, but they are all dry.

plies half of the world's oxygen, but since 1970, more than 60% of the rainforest has been cut down or burned to build roads or buildings. It doesn't take a genius, does it? No trees = no air = no animals and people.

A **grassland** is a big, wide-open area that's full of, well, grass. It usually separates a forest from a desert. The grassland has very few trees, and it's often windy and dry (but not as dry as a desert).

There are two kinds of **forest** biomes: a **deciduous forest** and a **taiga**. An easy way to remember the difference is: A tree in a deciduous forest loses its leaves (think *d*'s here—**d**eciduous **d**rops leaves), and taiga trees are always green (think Christmas trees). Deciduous forests are located between the equator and the poles. They have four seasons, causing the leaves to change colors. Taiga forests are located north of deciduous forests, in a cold climate with harsh winters. There are fewer animals in a taiga because of the weather.

A **rainforest** is a very wet forest with lots of different kinds of plants and animals. It is almost always raining in a rainforest. (Aha! That's why it's called a rainforest!) The Amazon in South America is the world's largest rainforest and is home to more species of animals and plants than any other place on Earth. The Amazon has one-third of the world's trees and sup-

A **tundra** is the coldest biome and is found near the North Pole. The ground of tundra is called **permafrost**, because it is almost always frozen ("perma" is comes from the word "permanent"). Very few plants or animals live here.

Other names for grassland are savanna, plain, prairie, and steppe.

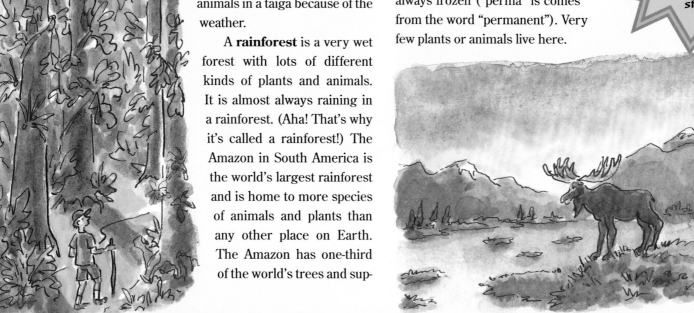

Biomes and Some Animals Who Live There:

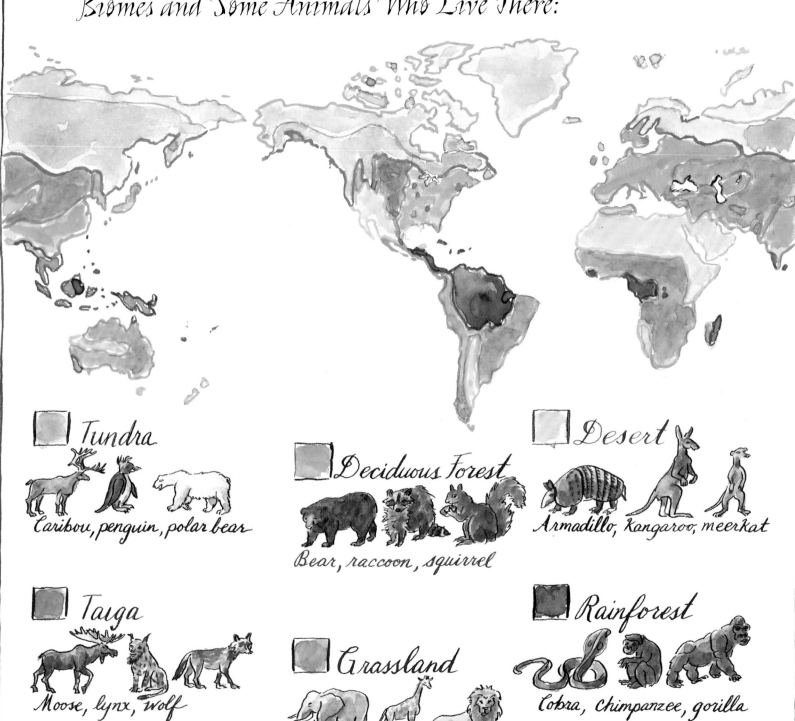

Tundra
Caribou, penguin, polar bear

Deciduous Forest
Bear, raccoon, squirrel

Desert
Armadillo, kangaroo, meerkat

Taiga
Moose, lynx, wolf

Grassland
Elephant, giraffe, lion

Rainforest
Cobra, chimpanzee, gorilla

It's Getting Crowded in Here

 ow many people live on Earth? Come on, pick a number. Let's see how close you are.

Geographers estimate there are over *6.8 billion people* on Earth.

Wow, that's a lot of people sharing one planet! Wait—no. Change that number, because *every single minute, 253 babies are born in the world . . .* and only a hundred people die in that same minute. *That's about 2.5 more people being born every minute than dying.* Every week we add a million and a half people to the world. The United Nations predicts the Earth's population will reach 9.2 billion by 2050.

Projected **POP**ulation Growth — in Billions

1950 1970 1990 2010 2030 2050

Where Did All These People Come From?

Until the 1800s, the population stayed pretty much the same (about 1 billion in 1850). Then—*whoosh!*—came medicine, better health, a food supply we could count on, more education, machines, and an overall better style of life. People lived longer. They had lots of babies, and the babies lived and grew up and had children. And so on and so on.

Going Global

LET'S SAY YOU ARE ONLINE AND YOU FIND A GREAT, NEW COMIC BOOK BEING SOLD BY A KID IN JAPAN. IF YOU WANT IT, YOU E-MAIL HIM A MESSAGE, SEND HIM THE MONEY, AND HE SHIPS YOU THE COMIC BOOK. THAT IS **GLOBAL-IZATION**—EVERYBODY AROUND THE WORLD WORKING TO-GETHER. NOT SO LONG AGO, ONLY KIDS IN JAPAN WOULD HAVE KNOWN ABOUT A COMIC BOOK MADE IN JAPAN. BE-FORE THE PHONE, THE INTERNET, OVERNIGHT SHIPPING, AND AIRPLANES, EVERY COUNTRY PRETTY MUCH STAYED TO ITSELF. TODAY, DIFFERENCES IN TIME, SPACE, AND EVEN LANGUAGE DON'T MATTER MUCH. EVERYONE IN THE WORLD IS CLOSER—WE KNOW MORE ABOUT OTHER CULTURES, WE CREATE PRODUCTS THAT ARE SOLD EVERYWHERE (MCDON-ALD®, NIKE®, COCA-COLA®), AND WE WATCH INTERNA-TIONAL SPORTS MATCHES AND EVENTS LIVE. SO IS GLO-BALIZATION GOOD? SOME PEOPLE SAY IT HAS MADE PEOPLE LESS POOR AND STOPPED WARS. OTHER PEOPLE THINK IT HAS WIPED AWAY THE TRADITIONAL CUSTOMS THAT MADE EACH COUNTRY SPECIAL. WHAT DO YOU THINK?

Where Do They All Live?

Asia is the most populated continent. Six out of every ten people live in Asia.

If a country is large, then you would think it would have a lot of people, right? Russia and Canada are two of the largest countries, so why aren't they on the list? True, Russia and Canada have a lot of land—but they don't have a lot of *land* that people actually want to live on. It's way too cold!

1.33 bil.

1.17 bil.

307 bil.

231 bil.

CHINA INDIA U.S. INDONESIA

Communities

People live in every continent except Antarctica, which is covered with ice. Some areas on Earth are really crowded, and some areas are totally empty. This is called the **population density,** or the number of people living in a square mile or square kilometer. Three types of communities are based on population density:

RURAL COMMUNITIES ARE OUT IN THE COUNTRY. THERE IS A LOT OF LAND AND THE BUILDINGS ARE FARTHER APART. THE POPULATION IS LOWER IN RURAL AREAS.

URBAN COMMUNITIES HAVE THE BIGGEST POPULATIONS. HALF OF THE PEOPLE IN THE WORLD LIVE IN AN URBAN ENVIRONMENT. URBAN AREAS ARE CITIES WITH BUILDINGS THAT ARE CLOSE TOGETHER, AND HAVE A BUS OR SUBWAY SYSTEM FOR TRANSPORTATION.

SUBURBAN COMMUNITIES ARE FOUND IN THE SMALLER TOWNS RIGHT OUTSIDE CITIES. MANY PEOPLE WHO LIVE IN THE SUBURBS WORK IN THE CITY.

What kind of community do you live in?

Not Enough to Go Around

You bring one friend home for dinner. Mom sets another place at the table.

You bring your whole class home for dinner. Mom's frazzled, but scrapes together enough food to feed everyone.

You bring your whole school home for dinner. Mom's in shock. Your family doesn't have enough food in the pantry to feed everyone. Kids go hungry.

Every environment can produce food and energy for only a certain number of people. If there are too many people, then certain animals and plants will die out because they are not given enough time to grow back before they are used for food. Most scientists believe that the Earth can only support between 8 and 11 billion people. So what's the answer?

A new way of life. *Conserve more and consume less.* Think of everything you've consumed or used in your life—all the food and the packaging around it, all the clothes and toys, all the video games and electronics, all the times you drove in a car and bus. All the energy, resources, and products you used came from the Earth, and all the waste is dumped back onto our planet. Our natural resources—our forests, our oceans, our rainforests—are being cut down and polluted so people can have more food, more buildings, more things. We are changing our planet and taking away things that won't ever come back. Instead, we all need to reuse products and create less waste, so we can be sure the Earth will be healthy for years and years.

Who We Are

hat did you eat for breakfast this morning? In the United States, you might have eaten eggs and cereal. In Japan, you might have eaten miso soup and rice. In Israel, you might have eaten cucumbers and tomatoes. In Australia, you might have eaten toast topped with spaghetti.

Much of who you are and how you act (and what you eat) comes from your **culture**. Culture is your way of life. People around the world all eat, sleep, and communicate—but we eat different foods, sleep in different types of places, and talk in different languages. Our culture is what makes us different. Culture is what sets one group of people apart from another group. In addition to food, shelter, and language, a culture shares art, music, stories, inventions, celebrations, beliefs, and customs.

All culture is learned. Were you born knowing how to shake hands or bow when greeting someone? Did you know how to speak English or Farsi right away? No—you

Greetings from Around the World

HOW PEOPLE SAY HELLO IS A CULTURAL THING. THERE'S NO RIGHT WAY TO DO IT. WHAT IS CONSIDERED NICE IN ONE CULTURE CAN OFTEN BE SEEN AS RUDE OR STRANGE IN ANOTHER.

Belgium: PEOPLE GREET ONE ANOTHER WITH THREE KISSES GOING FROM CHEEK TO CHEEK.

Benin: YOUNG MEN OFTEN SNAP FINGERS WHILE SHAKING HANDS.

India: PEOPLE WHO PRACTICE THE HINDU RELIGION PRESS THEIR PALMS TOGETHER AS IF PRAYING, NOD THEIR HEADS, AND SAY, "NAMASTE."

Japan: PEOPLE GREET ONE ANOTHER BY BOWING LOW AT THE WAIST.

Korea: PEOPLE BOW ONLY SLIGHTLY.

Mozambique: IN THE NORTHERN PART OF THIS COUNTRY, MANY PEOPLE CLAP THEIR HANDS THREE TIMES BEFORE SAYING, "HELLO."

New Zealand: THE MAORI TRIBES RUB NOSES TOGETHER.

Somalia: INSTEAD OF SAYING, "GOOD MORNING," PEOPLE SAY, "HAVE YOU BEEN IN PEACE DURING THE NIGHT?"

Thailand: PEOPLE PLACE THEIR HANDS IN A PRAYING POSITION BY THEIR CHEST. THE HIGHER YOUR HANDS, THE MORE RESPECT YOU HAVE FOR THE PERSON YOU ARE GREETING. BUT, WATCH OUT—PLACING YOUR HANDS ABOVE YOUR HEAD IS AN INSULT.

United States: PEOPLE SHAKE HANDS, LOOK IN THE OTHER PERSON'S EYES, AND SAY, "HELLO."

Happy Birthday!

What's the best holiday? Your birthday, of course! Birthdays are one of the few holidays that are celebrated by almost everyone in every country. Many kids around the world have cakes, candles, and birthday songs, but there are also other cultural birthday traditions.

Argentina: When a girl turns fifteen, she dances a waltz with her father.

Brazil: The birthday child gets a pull on the earlobe for every year he or she has been alive.

Canada: In the eastern part of Canada, the birthday child is chased and, when caught, his or her nose is greased with butter for good luck.

China: The birthday child is served a bowl of noodles for lunch.

Denmark: A flag is flown outside the house to show that someone inside is having a birthday that day.

India: On her birthday, a girl wears a colored dress to school and passes out chocolates.

Japan: On his or her birthday, a child wears all new clothes.

Mexico: A piñata, made out of papier-mâché, is hung up and the birthday child hits it with a stick until it breaks and candies and gifts tumble out.

Nepal: A mixture of rice yogurt and color is placed on the birthday child's forehead for good luck.

Russia: Instead of cake, many children have birthday pies.

Vietnam: Everyone's birthday is celebrated on New Year's Day, which is called "Tet."

learned from your family, your teachers, or others who live close by. Culture is passed on from one generation to the next.

Your culture usually comes from the country you live in or the country where your parents, grandparents, or great-grandparents were born. If you live in the United States, your culture would be American. But what if your grandparents were from Ireland and they still made you Irish foods and sang Irish songs? Then you would have a subculture—or second culture—and would call yourself Irish-American. Today, even though so many people move around the world, they often keep many of their original cultural traditions. What is your family's culture?

The most common last name in the world is Chang.

Part 2

WELCOME TO THE WORLD

The Continents

Now that you've got a feel for the land and the water and all the environmental stuff that makes the Earth, well, the Earth, let's take a closer look at each of the seven continents.

A **continent** is described as an unbroken landmass completely surrounded by water. Do you like that definition? Check out the map. What about Europe? Europe looks like it's a part of Asia. There are some geographers who say they are really one continent called **Eurasia**. And what about North America and South America—shouldn't they be one continent? It may not make a whole lot of sense, but most scientists and geographers agree we have seven continents . . . so, seven it is.

Every continent has many countries (except Antarctica, which has just Antarctica). A **country** is an area ruled by one government. It is independent, meaning another country does not make rules for it. Right now, **there are 195 independent countries in the world**.

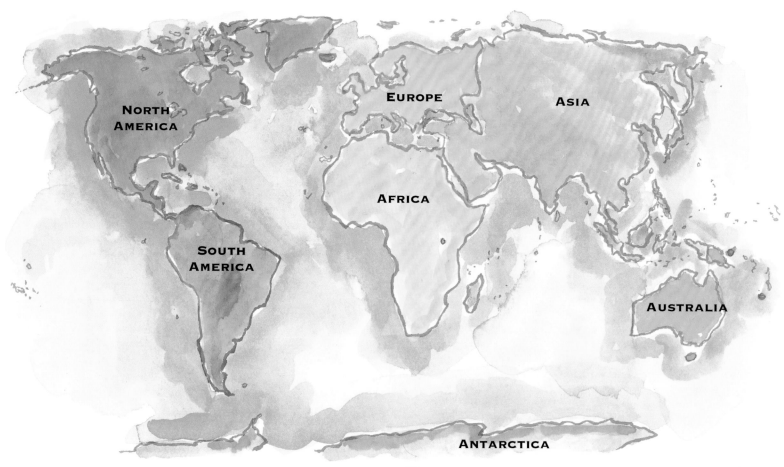

NORTH AMERICA

EUROPE

ASIA

AFRICA

SOUTH AMERICA

AUSTRALIA

ANTARCTICA

Countries come in all different shapes and sizes. The three biggest countries in the world are: Russia, Canada, and the United States. The three smallest are: Vatican City, Monaco, and Nauru.

Some areas that may look like a country really aren't. They are called **dependent territories**. To "depend" means "to rely on someone else." These territories don't have full independence. They rely on a bigger, more powerful country for governing, protection, and aid.

Cities are found in every country. A city is an urban area with lots of people and businesses. Cities come in all different sizes. New York City is one of the largest cities in the world in **area**, or how much land it takes up. Mumbai, India, is the city with the largest population. Hum, Croatia, is said to be the smallest city, with less than twenty people living there—that's probably about the same number of kids in your class!

Now it's time for a spelling lesson.

- A **capital** is a *city* that is the center of a country's government.
- A **capitol** is a *building* in the capital where the people in the government meet.

*You often find a capit**O**l in a capit**A**l!*

It's all about the vowels, my friend.

And then, of course, there are towns and villages. Most people say a town is larger than a village, but smaller than a city.

Your Side of the Line

On a map, a line separates two countries or two cities. This is called a **border**. But when you're driving in your car and your mom says, "We've just left France, and now we're in Belgium," why don't you see the thick black border line on the street? Well, there are two kinds of borders: a **natural** border and a **political** border.

- A natural border is something in nature, such as a river, an ocean, or a mountain range, that divides two areas. For example, the Rhine (a river) naturally separates Germany from Switzerland.

Natural Border   Political Border

- A political border is an agreed-upon imaginary line on a map. An example is the United States' border with Canada (or the line your mom makes down the car seat to stop you and your siblings from fighting!).

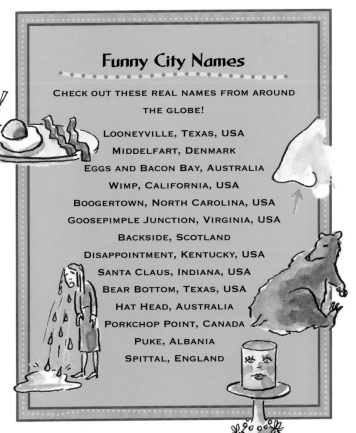

Funny City Names

CHECK OUT THESE REAL NAMES FROM AROUND THE GLOBE!

LOONEYVILLE, TEXAS, USA
MIDDELFART, DENMARK
EGGS AND BACON BAY, AUSTRALIA
WIMP, CALIFORNIA, USA
BOOGERTOWN, NORTH CAROLINA, USA
GOOSEPIMPLE JUNCTION, VIRGINIA, USA
BACKSIDE, SCOTLAND
DISAPPOINTMENT, KENTUCKY, USA
SANTA CLAUS, INDIANA, USA
BEAR BOTTOM, TEXAS, USA
HAT HEAD, AUSTRALIA
PORKCHOP POINT, CANADA
PUKE, ALBANIA
SPITTAL, ENGLAND

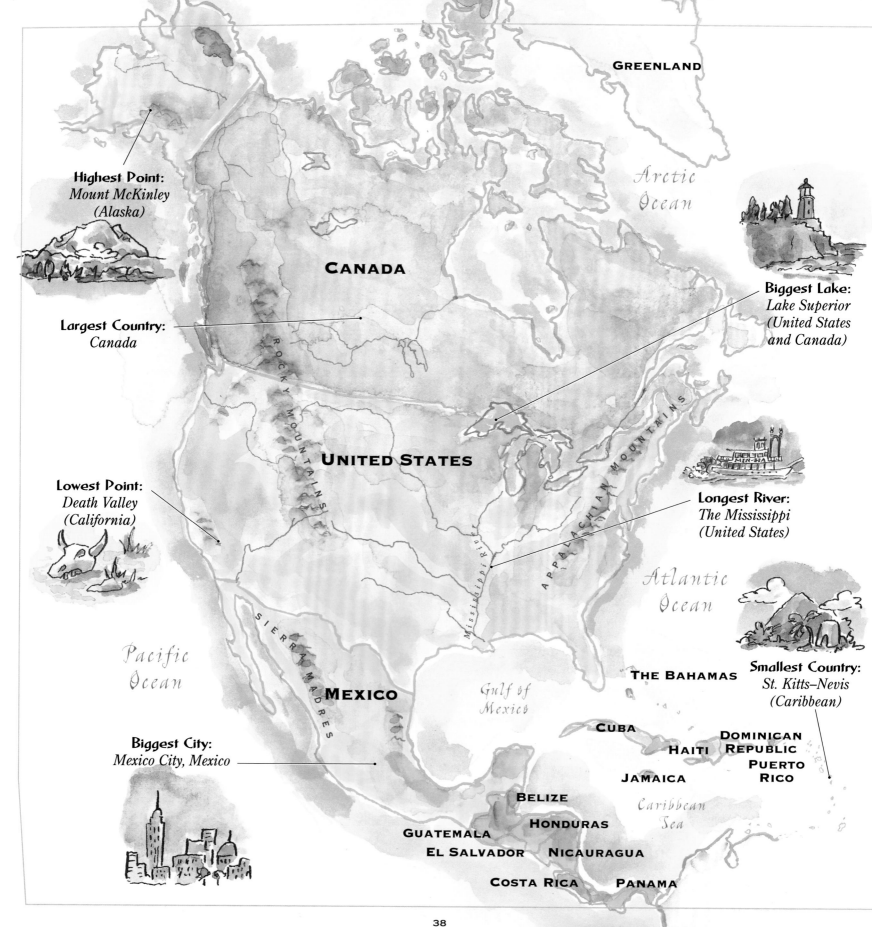

GREENLAND

Arctic Ocean

CANADA

Highest Point:
*Mount McKinley
(Alaska)*

Largest Country:
Canada

Biggest Lake:
*Lake Superior
(United States
and Canada)*

ROCKY MOUNTAINS

APPALACHIAN MOUNTAINS

UNITED STATES

Lowest Point:
*Death Valley
(California)*

Longest River:
*The Mississippi
(United States)*

Mississippi River

Atlantic Ocean

Pacific Ocean

SIERRA MADRES

MEXICO

*Gulf of
Mexico*

THE BAHAMAS

Smallest Country:
*St. Kitts–Nevis
(Caribbean)*

Biggest City:
Mexico City, Mexico

CUBA

HAITI

**DOMINICAN
REPUBLIC**

**PUERTO
RICO**

JAMAICA

*Caribbean
Sea*

BELIZE

HONDURAS

GUATEMALA

EL SALVADOR

NICAURAGUA

COSTA RICA

PANAMA

North America is the third-largest continent, but for a long time, the rest of the world didn't know it existed. Of course, millions of native people were living there—but no one knew that. When the European explorers finally sailed the ocean blue and bumped into this huge piece of land, they called it "the New World." North America has since grown to become one of the most advanced and wealthiest continents on the planet.

North America is home to the United States, Canada, Mexico, Central America, the Caribbean Islands, and Greenland. The continent is bracketed by the Atlantic Ocean on its east side and the Pacific Ocean on its west side. The **Rocky Mountains** reach over 3,000 miles (4,828 km)—from Alaska into Canada down through the western United States and into New Mexico. The Rockies are young mountains, so their snow-covered peaks are sharp and jagged.

North America was settled by **immigrants**. An immigrant is someone who moves to a new country. Most immigrants came to North America from Europe and Asia to find freedom and for the chance at a better life for themselves and their families. But not all people chose to come here. Many black Americans were brought over from Africa as slaves, from about 1619 to 1808. Slavery was finally stopped in 1865.

HOW AMERICA GOT ITS NAME

Why is America called America? It's all because of a German mapmaker named Martin Waldseemuller. He was the first mapmaker to say that Columbus hadn't reached Asia but had discovered an uncharted territory. He made a map in 1507, showing the new land, and he named it "America" to honor Amerigo Vespucci, an Italian explorer who had sailed to the New World after Columbus. Even though Columbus got there first, Vespucci was aware he was in a "New World" and not Asia. Waldseemuller's map became very popular (this was right around the time the printing press was invented, so people were into making copies of things). Soon people all over Europe were calling the New World "America." Years later, Waldseemuller said he had made a mistake and should have named the New World after Columbus. But by then, it was too late—everyone liked the name America.

Nina, Pinta, Santa Maria

"COLUMBUS-ERICA" would have been fairer...

The United States of America

The **United States of America** (USA) is a huge country, and because it is so large, it is broken into fifty smaller parts, or **states**. The states and its people live under the laws and rules of the United States. Each state makes its own local laws, and it sends **representatives** to speak for it in the national government (the same way your class may choose a student to represent your class in the school government or council).

The United States stretches across North America. When people talk about the **continental United States**, they mean the forty-eight states that lie between Canada to the north and Mexico to the south, and from the Atlantic Ocean to the east to the Pacific Ocean to the west (that's where "from sea to shining sea" comes from!). Alaska and Hawaii are not attached to all the other states. Alaska is by northwest Canada, and Hawaii is a chain of volcanic islands in the Pacific Ocean. The United States is so large it covers six time zones.

The capital of the United States is **Washington DC**, which is on the banks of the Potomac River between the states of Virginia and Maryland. DC stands for District of Columbia. Washington DC is a city. It is neither a state nor within a state, because the nation's early lawmakers decided it was best to have the nation's capital be separate and not part of any one state. The United States is a **democracy** (which means every adult gets a vote), and every four years it elects a president. The president lives in the **White House**. The United States declared its independence from Great Britain on July 4, 1776.

ALASKA

Pacific Ocean

Not Attached!

THE BALD EAGLE IS THE OFFICIAL SYMBOL OF THE UNITED STATES. IT WAS CHOSEN, IN 1782, BECAUSE MANY THOUGHT THE EAGLE'S WIDE WINGSPAN REPRESENTED FREEDOM. DID YOU KNOW THAT BENJAMIN FRANKLIN, ONE OF THE UNITED STATES' FOUNDING FATHERS, WANTED THE TURKEY TO BE THE NATIONAL SYMBOL INSTEAD OF THE EAGLE?

If Ben Franklin had had HIS way...

What You Need to Know about the United States

MAIN CROPS: WHEAT, CORN, HAY, SOYBEANS, POTATOES, TOMATOES, COTTON

SOME NATIVE ANIMALS: BEAR, DEER, WOLF, RACCOON, PRAIRIE DOG

MAIN LANGUAGES: ENGLISH, SPANISH

CULTURAL HOLIDAYS: INDEPENDENCE DAY, THANKSGIVING, MEMORIAL DAY, MARTIN LUTHER KING DAY

FAVORITE SPORTS: BASEBALL, FOOTBALL, BASKETBALL

FAVORITE FOODS: APPLE PIE, HAMBURGERS AND HOT DOGS, SOURDOUGH BREAD, FRIED CHICKEN

INVENTIONS: AIRPLANE, ARTIFICIAL HEART, COMPUTER, THE INTERNET, AIR-CONDITIONING, REFRIGERATOR

HELLO! Hola!

CASCADE MOUNTAINS

OREGO

SIERRA NEVADA MO

CALIFORN

HAWAII

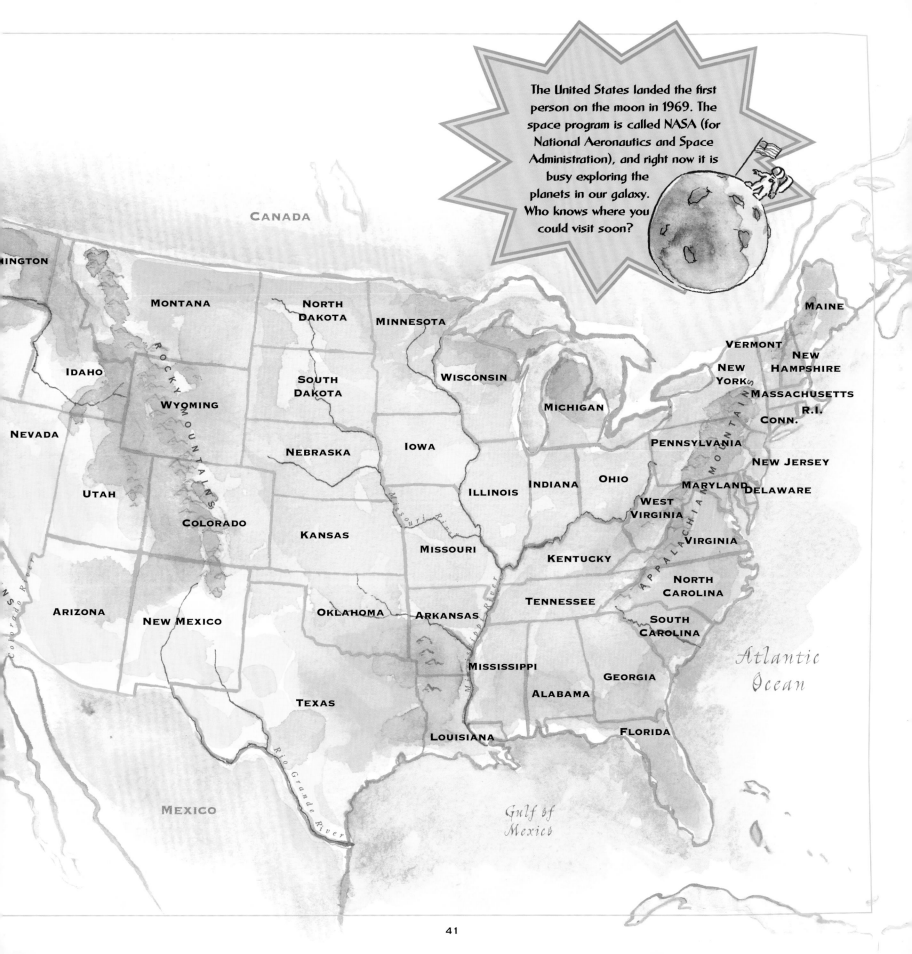

The United States landed the first person on the moon in 1969. The space program is called NASA (for National Aeronautics and Space Administration), and right now it is busy exploring the planets in our galaxy. Who knows where you could visit soon?

CANADA

WASHINGTON

MONTANA

NORTH DAKOTA

MINNESOTA

MAINE

IDAHO

SOUTH DAKOTA

WISCONSIN

VERMONT

NEW HAMPSHIRE

NEW YORK

MASSACHUSETTS

R.I.

CONN.

WYOMING

MICHIGAN

ROCKY MOUNTAINS

NEVADA

NEBRASKA

IOWA

PENNSYLVANIA

NEW JERSEY

UTAH

ILLINOIS

INDIANA

OHIO

MARYLAND

DELAWARE

WEST VIRGINIA

COLORADO

KANSAS

Missouri River

MISSOURI

KENTUCKY

VIRGINIA

APPALACHIAN MOUNTAINS

NORTH CAROLINA

ARIZONA

NEW MEXICO

OKLAHOMA

ARKANSAS

Mississippi River

TENNESSEE

SOUTH CAROLINA

Atlantic Ocean

Colorado River

MISSISSIPPI

GEORGIA

TEXAS

ALABAMA

LOUISIANA

FLORIDA

Rio Grande River

MEXICO

Gulf of Mexico

KNOW YOUR APPALACHIAN MOUNTAINS

The Appalachian Mountains run from Canada all the way down to Alabama. They are some of the oldest mountains in the world. Their tops are worn down due to years and years of erosion. Many other mountain chains are part of the Appalachians:

THE **ADIRONDACK MOUNTAINS** AND **CATSKILL MOUNTAINS** IN **NEW YORK**

THE **BLUE RIDGE MOUNTAINS** FROM **PENNSYLVANIA** DOWN THROUGH **GEORGIA**

THE **GREEN MOUNTAINS** IN **VERMONT** AND THE **WHITE MOUNTAINS** IN **NEW HAMPSHIRE**

THE **GREAT SMOKY MOUNTAINS** ON THE **TENNESSEE-NORTH CAROLINA** BORDER

YOU CAN WALK THE **APPALACHIAN TRAIL** FROM MAINE TO GEORGIA. WEAR GOOD SHOES— IT'S 2,000 MILES!

THE **DECLARATION OF INDEPENDENCE** WAS SIGNED IN **PHILADELPHIA, PENNSYLVANIA.**

CANADA

MAINE

VERMONT
Montpelier

Augusta ★

NEW HAMPSHIRE

Concord ★

Lake Ontario

Albany ★

Boston

MASSACHUSETTS

NEW YORK

CONN.

R.I.

Providence

Hartford

PENNSYLVANIA

Harrisburg

Trenton ★

NEW JERSEY

MARYLAND

Annapolis

Dover ★

DELAWARE

WEST VIRGINIA

Charleston ★

WASHINGTON, DC IS THE NATIONAL CAPITOL. FAMOUS MONUMENTS ARE THE CAPITOL, THE WASHINGTON MONUMENT, AND THE LINCOLN MEMORIAL.

MAMMOTH CAVE IN KENTUCKY IS THE LARGEST SYSTEM OF CAVES IN THE WORLD.

Frankfort ★

Richmond ★

KENTUCKY

VIRGINIA

Nashville ★

Raleigh ★

NORTH CAROLINA

TENNESSEE

SOUTH CAROLINA

Columbia ★

Atlantic Ocean

ATLANTA, GEORGIA IS WHERE COCA-COLA WAS INVENTED AND WHERE CIVIL RIGHTS LEADER MARTIN LUTHER KING JR. WAS BORN.

★ *Atlanta*

MISSISSIPPI

GEORGIA

Mississippi River

Montgomery ★

LOUISIANA

Jackson ★

ALABAMA

THE OKEFENOKEE SWAMP ON THE GEORGIA-FLORIDA BORDER IS ONE OF THE LARGEST SWAMPS IN THE WORLD.

Baton Rouge ★

Tallahassee ★

FLORIDA

You should have seen the one that got away...

Gulf of Mexico

NEW ORLEANS IS KNOWN AS THE BIRTHPLACE OF JAZZ MUSIC, AND IT HOSTS A WILD MARDI GRAS CELEBRATION EVERY YEAR.

THE GULF OF MEXICO IS THE WORLD'S LARGEST GULF. THE GULF'S WARM WATERS, WHICH FLOW INTO THE ATLANTIC OCEAN AND THE CARIBBEAN SEA, MAKE IT A GREAT SPOT FOR FISHING.

ORLANDO, FLORIDA ALWAYS HAS LOTS OF VISITORS AT WALT DISNEY WORLD.

Eastern United States

BOSTON, MASSACHUSETTS IS FAMOUS FOR THE REVOLUTIONARY WAR'S BOSTON TEA PARTY.

TAKE THAT, BRITISH!

NEW YORK CITY, WITH ITS ENORMOUS SKYSCRAPERS, IS THE LARGEST CITY IN THE USA AND IS ALSO KNOWN AS THE FINANCIAL CAPITAL OF THE WORLD. THE UNITED NATIONS, AN ORGANIZATION OF COUNTRIES THAT WORKS FOR WORLDWIDE PEACE, IS LOCATED HERE.

New York City is often called, "The Melting Pot," because so many people from so many countries live here. About 40% of NYC population was born in a different country.

THE EVERGLADES IS A PROTECTED WETLAND THAT RUNS ACROSS THE SOUTHERN TIP OF FLORIDA. ALLIGATORS AND CROCODILES LIVE HERE PLUS, HUNDREDS OF OTHER PLANTS AND ANIMALS, AS WELL AS THE ENDANGERED FLORIDA PANTHER.

The eastern **United States** was the first part of the country to be settled by the European explorers and is home to the country's original thirteen colonies. It's a very busy, busy area. It's the most populated part of the country with many bustling cities, such as Washington DC, Boston, New York City, Philadelphia, Atlanta, and Miami. Many businesses and companies are located on the East Coast.

The eastern United States runs from Maine, up north next to Canada, over the Appalachian Mountains and down south to the Gulf Coast and the beaches of Florida. The states in the northeastern corner have rocky, jagged coastlines and beautiful harbors for fishing and catching lobsters. Farther south, the beaches along the coast are sandy. The fertile lands in the east are good for farming, especially vegetable and fruit crops. The southernmost states are often known as the "cotton states," because before the war between the Northern and Southern states, cotton was a huge crop grown on big farms, called **plantations**. The tropical climates and the low lands of Florida, Mississippi, and Alabama have created many swamps and **bayous**. A bayou is a slow-moving stream in a swamp.

Holiday Highlight

THANKSGIVING IS ONE OF THE MOST IMPORTANT HOLIDAYS IN THE UNITED STATES. AFTER THE PILGRIMS' FIRST HARD WINTER IN AMERICA IN 1622, THEIR CROPS FINALLY CAME IN, AND THEY SHARED A FEAST WITH THE NATIVE AMERICANS TO GIVE THANKS. TODAY, KIDS ALL ACROSS THE USA EAT A BIG MEAL OF TURKEY, STUFFING, CRANBERRY SAUCE, AND PUMPKIN PIE WITH THEIR FAMILIES ON THE FOURTH THURSDAY IN NOVEMBER.

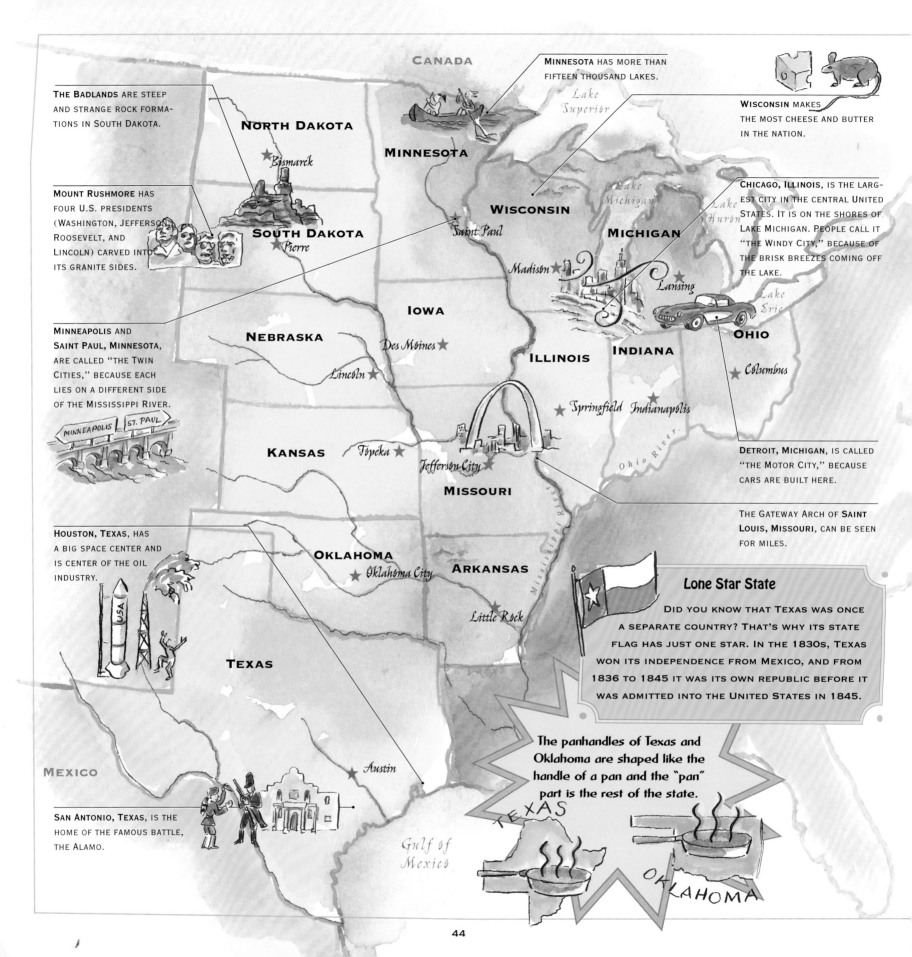

CANADA

MINNESOTA HAS MORE THAN FIFTEEN THOUSAND LAKES.

Lake Superior

WISCONSIN MAKES THE MOST CHEESE AND BUTTER IN THE NATION.

THE BADLANDS ARE STEEP AND STRANGE ROCK FORMATIONS IN SOUTH DAKOTA.

NORTH DAKOTA

★ *Bismarck*

MINNESOTA

Lake Michigan

WISCONSIN

★ *Saint Paul*

MICHIGAN

Lake Huron

CHICAGO, ILLINOIS, IS THE LARGEST CITY IN THE CENTRAL UNITED STATES. IT IS ON THE SHORES OF LAKE MICHIGAN. PEOPLE CALL IT "THE WINDY CITY," BECAUSE OF THE BRISK BREEZES COMING OFF THE LAKE.

MOUNT RUSHMORE HAS FOUR U.S. PRESIDENTS (WASHINGTON, JEFFERSON ROOSEVELT, AND LINCOLN) CARVED INTO ITS GRANITE SIDES.

SOUTH DAKOTA

★ *Pierre*

IOWA

Madison ★

★ *Lansing*

Lake Erie

OHIO

MINNEAPOLIS AND SAINT PAUL, MINNESOTA, ARE CALLED "THE TWIN CITIES," BECAUSE EACH LIES ON A DIFFERENT SIDE OF THE MISSISSIPPI RIVER.

NEBRASKA

★ *Des Moines*

INDIANA

★ *Columbus*

ILLINOIS

★ *Lincoln*

KANSAS

★ *Topeka*

★ *Springfield* *Indianapolis* ★

Ohio River

Jefferson City ★

MISSOURI

DETROIT, MICHIGAN, IS CALLED "THE MOTOR CITY," BECAUSE CARS ARE BUILT HERE.

HOUSTON, TEXAS, HAS A BIG SPACE CENTER AND IS CENTER OF THE OIL INDUSTRY.

OKLAHOMA

★ *Oklahoma City*

ARKANSAS

Mississippi River

THE GATEWAY ARCH OF SAINT LOUIS, MISSOURI, CAN BE SEEN FOR MILES.

★ *Little Rock*

Lone Star State

DID YOU KNOW THAT TEXAS WAS ONCE A SEPARATE COUNTRY? THAT'S WHY ITS STATE FLAG HAS JUST ONE STAR. IN THE 1830S, TEXAS WON ITS INDEPENDENCE FROM MEXICO, AND FROM 1836 TO 1845 IT WAS ITS OWN REPUBLIC BEFORE IT WAS ADMITTED INTO THE UNITED STATES IN 1845.

TEXAS

The panhandles of Texas and Oklahoma are shaped like the handle of a pan and the "pan" part is the rest of the state.

MEXICO

★ *Austin*

SAN ANTONIO, TEXAS, IS THE HOME OF THE FAMOUS BATTLE, THE ALAMO.

Gulf of Mexico

TEXAS

OKLAHOMA

Central United States

The central United States sits right in the middle of the country. Much of this area is flat prairie, and it's often called "the Great Plains." The rich soil is perfect for farming. Most of the country's grain (wheat and corn—the stuff used to bake bread and make cereal) is grown here, giving this area another nickname— "the Breadbasket."

The middle of the country has two big waterways. The **Mississippi River** runs from Minnesota in the north down to the Gulf of Mexico. It is the country's busiest waterway. **The Great Lakes** are five lakes that sit on the United States/Canada border and contain one-fifth of the world's freshwater. Lake Michigan is the only one of the Great Lakes that's entirely in the United States. The five lakes are linked together by waterways and all drain into the Saint Lawrence River, which empties into the Atlantic Ocean. A trick to remember the names of the Great Lakes is the word HOMES (**Huron, Ontario, Michigan, Erie, Superior**).

The large, open plains of Texas and Oklahoma are perfect for raising beef cattle. Cowboys herd the cattle on huge farms, called **ranches**. Texas is also known for oil. The eastern part of the state pumps the most oil in the country, except for Alaska.

TORNADO ALLEY

A tornado or a twister is an intense column of wind that comes with a thunderstorm (just like the wind that blew Dorothy and her house to Munchkin Land in *The Wizard of Oz*). Most tornadoes in the USA happen in an area called "tornado alley," which covers Texas, Oklahoma, Kansas, and Nebraska. Here, the flatlands allow the cold air from Canada and the warm air from the Gulf of Mexico to collide during spring and summer storms. The air churns together and creates a powerful swirling wind that can knock over buildings and toss cars off roads.

Western United States

Welcome to the Wild West! The West is all about the great outdoors—towering mountains, parched deserts, deep canyons, and thick forests with enormous trees. It is the land of cowboys and pioneers who settled the frontier.

The western United States covers the most land in the country, from the Rocky Mountains all the way to the Pacific Ocean. The Rockies are hundreds of miles wide and its tallest peaks are in Colorado. Two other mountain ranges, the majestic Cascade Mountains and Sierra Nevada Mountains, rise up by the Pacific coast. The Cascades are volcanic mountains. Mount Saint Helens in Washington erupted about thirty years ago.

In Arizona, New Mexico, Nevada, California, and Utah, the landscape changes to desert. The two main deserts are the Mojave and the Sonora. The Mojave Desert in Southern California is America's largest desert and home to Death Valley, the lowest (and hottest!) point in the Western Hemisphere. The southwest of the United States once belonged to Mexico, and you can see Mexican influence in the architecture and food.

The beauty of the West continues with the enormous redwood and sequoia trees grown along the coasts of California, Oregon, and Washington. The redwood trees can reach over 300 feet (92 m)—that's the length of eight yellow school buses!

What Is a Volcano?

A VOLCANO IS A MOUNTAIN THAT HAS A POOL OF MOLTEN ROCK (**MAGMA**) UNDER ITS SURFACE. WHEN PRESSURE INSIDE EARTH BUILDS UP AND THE TECTONIC PLATES SHIFT, A VOLCANO ERUPTS. GAS AND BURNING ROCK (CALLED **LAVA**) SHOOT OUT. THERE ARE OVER FIVE HUNDRED ACTIVE VOLCANOES IN THE WORLD. THE **RING OF FIRE** IS AN AREA THAT CIRCLES THE PACIFIC OCEAN AND CONTAINS MOST OF THE ACTIVE VOLCANOES.

LEWIS AND CLARK GO WEST

In 1803, when Thomas Jefferson was president, the United States bought all the land west of the Mississippi from France. This was called "the Louisiana Purchase." After he handed France the money, Jefferson got nervous. What did he just buy? He had absolutely no idea. Maps of the West were blank. Jefferson sent Meriwether Lewis and William Clark to explore the wilds of the west. He instructed them to map the rivers, make friends with the natives, and find a northwest passage—an overland water route across North America. Lewis and Clark started in Saint Charles, Missouri, and traveled to Oregon's coast and back again. They brought along a crew of men and a Native American woman named Sacagawea and her baby son. Sacagawea was very helpful, because she could speak with the chiefs of the tribes they met along the way. The journey took over two years and covered 8,000 miles (12,875 km). Clark, a cartographer, made 140 maps of the West. Lewis and Clark found three hundred unknown species of plants and animals, the Rocky Mountains, and fifty tribes of Native Americans. Even though a northwest passage was never found, Jefferson realized he had gotten good deal.

Pacific Ocean

Missouri

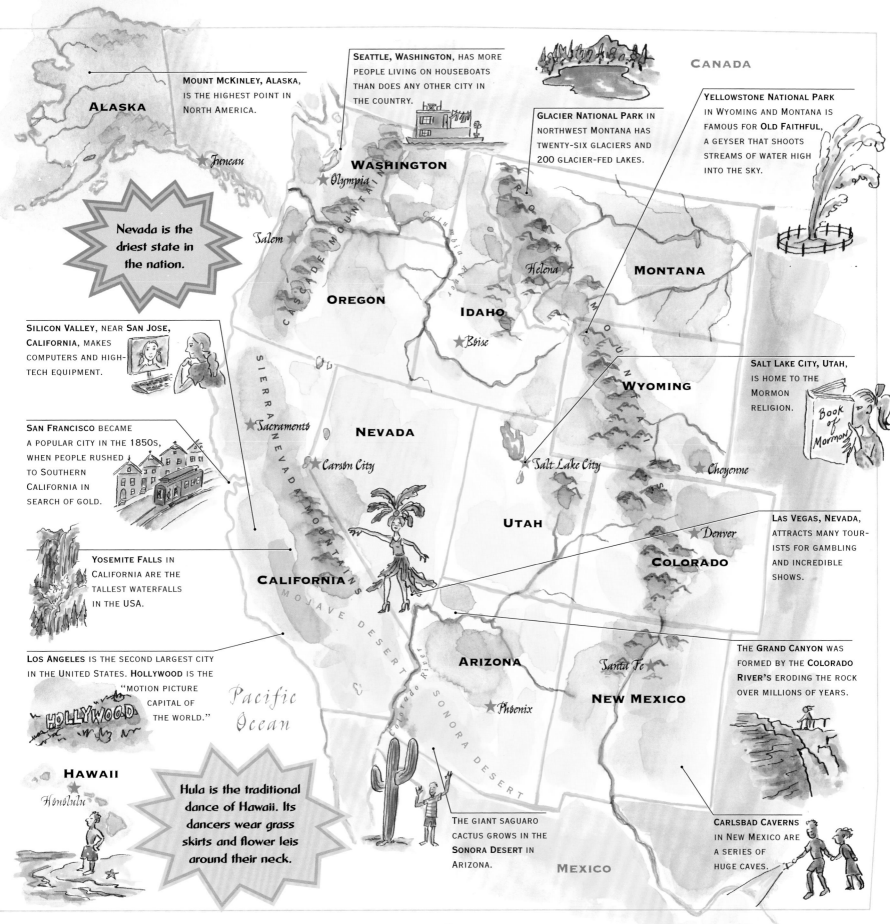

MOUNT McKINLEY, ALASKA, IS THE HIGHEST POINT IN NORTH AMERICA.

ALASKA

Juneau

SEATTLE, WASHINGTON, HAS MORE PEOPLE LIVING ON HOUSEBOATS THAN DOES ANY OTHER CITY IN THE COUNTRY.

WASHINGTON

Olympia

GLACIER NATIONAL PARK IN NORTHWEST MONTANA HAS TWENTY-SIX GLACIERS AND 200 GLACIER-FED LAKES.

CANADA

YELLOWSTONE NATIONAL PARK IN WYOMING AND MONTANA IS FAMOUS FOR OLD FAITHFUL, A GEYSER THAT SHOOTS STREAMS OF WATER HIGH INTO THE SKY.

Nevada is the driest state in the nation.

Salem

OREGON

CASCADE MOUNTAINS

Columbia River

Helena

MONTANA

IDAHO

Boise

SILICON VALLEY, NEAR SAN JOSE, CALIFORNIA, MAKES COMPUTERS AND HIGH-TECH EQUIPMENT.

WYOMING

SALT LAKE CITY, UTAH, IS HOME TO THE MORMON RELIGION.

Book of Mormon

SIERRA NEVADA MOUNTAINS

Sacramento

NEVADA

SAN FRANCISCO BECAME A POPULAR CITY IN THE 1850s, WHEN PEOPLE RUSHED TO SOUTHERN CALIFORNIA IN SEARCH OF GOLD.

Carson City

Salt Lake City

Cheyenne

UTAH

YOSEMITE FALLS IN CALIFORNIA ARE THE TALLEST WATERFALLS IN THE USA.

Denver

COLORADO

LAS VEGAS, NEVADA, ATTRACTS MANY TOURISTS FOR GAMBLING AND INCREDIBLE SHOWS.

CALIFORNIA

MOJAVE DESERT

LOS ANGELES IS THE SECOND LARGEST CITY IN THE UNITED STATES. HOLLYWOOD IS THE "MOTION PICTURE CAPITAL OF THE WORLD."

HOLLYWOOD

Pacific Ocean

Colorado River

ARIZONA

SONORA DESERT

Santa Fe

Phoenix

NEW MEXICO

THE GRAND CANYON WAS FORMED BY THE COLORADO RIVER'S ERODING THE ROCK OVER MILLIONS OF YEARS.

HAWAII

Honolulu

Hula is the traditional dance of Hawaii. Its dancers wear grass skirts and flower leis around their neck.

THE GIANT SAGUARO CACTUS GROWS IN THE SONORA DESERT IN ARIZONA.

CARLSBAD CAVERNS IN NEW MEXICO ARE A SERIES OF HUGE CAVES.

MEXICO

Canada

T he word "Canada" comes from a Huron Indian word, *kanata*, which means "small village." That's pretty funny because Canada is the world's second-largest country in size (only Russia is larger).

How Big Is Canada?

It's so big it takes up half the Northern Hemisphere.

It's so big it's surrounded by three oceans—the Atlantic, the Pacific, and the Arctic—giving it the longest coastline of any country.

It's so big it has the longest highway system in the world: the Trans-Canada Highway.

It's so big it covers six time zones.

Canada is divided into ten **provinces** and three territories. A province is just like a state in the United States—it has a local government and it sends representatives to vote on national laws. A territory does not have a local government and cannot vote on national laws (basically, it has no power). The territories (Yukon, Northwest Territories, Nunavut) reach way up north into the Arctic Circle.

The northernmost part of Canada, by the Arctic Circle, is tundra and stays frozen for about nine months of the year. Very few people live up here. The **Canadian Shield** is a hilly area of rivers and lakes that covers the northern part of the country. This is where some of the oldest rocks in the world have been found (we're talking rock that's 3.6 billion years old!). The Rocky Mountains and Coast Mountains reach across the western part of Canada, and there are lots of ranches and farms there. The southern part of Canada is the most populated. Nearly all Canada's main cities are close to the border with its only neighbor, the United States. The eastern provinces are known as the Maritime Provinces because they are surrounded by the ocean.

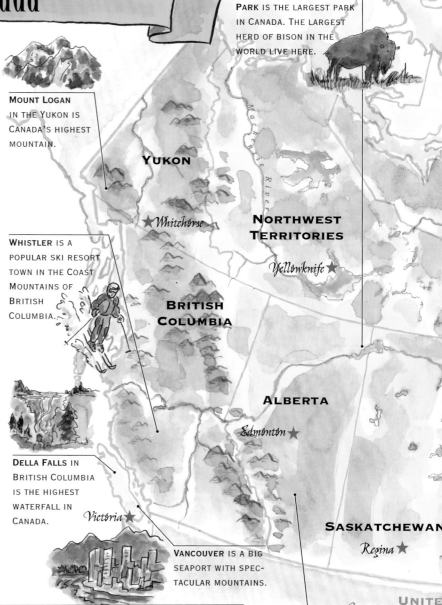

WOOD BUFFALO NATIONAL PARK IS THE LARGEST PARK IN CANADA. THE LARGEST HERD OF BISON IN THE WORLD LIVE HERE.

MOUNT LOGAN IN THE YUKON IS CANADA'S HIGHEST MOUNTAIN.

WHISTLER IS A POPULAR SKI RESORT TOWN IN THE COAST MOUNTAINS OF BRITISH COLUMBIA.

DELLA FALLS IN BRITISH COLUMBIA IS THE HIGHEST WATERFALL IN CANADA.

VANCOUVER IS A BIG SEAPORT WITH SPECTACULAR MOUNTAINS.

CALGARY IS AN OLD COWBOY TOWN, AND EVERY YEAR THEY HOLD THE CALGARY STAMPEDE TO CELEBRATE THEIR WILD WEST HERITAGE.

YUKON · Whitehorse · NORTHWEST TERRITORIES · Yellowknife · BRITISH COLUMBIA · Victoria · ALBERTA · Edmonton · SASKATCHEWAN · Regina · UNITE

What You Need to Know about Canada

MAIN CROPS: WHEAT, FLAX, BARLEY, SUGAR BEETS

SOME NATIVE ANIMALS: BEAVER, CANADA GOOSE, CARIBOU, MOOSE, WALRUS

MAIN LANGUAGES: ENGLISH, EXCEPT IN THE PROVINCE OF QUEBEC, WHERE FRENCH IS SPOKEN.

CULTURAL HOLIDAYS: CANADA DAY, NATIONAL ABORIGINAL DAY, SAINT-JEAN-BAPTISTE DAY, VICTORIA DAY

FAVORITE SPORTS: HOCKEY, LACROSSE, SKIING

FAVORITE FOODS: MAPLE SYRUP, CANADIAN BACON, SALMON

INVENTIONS: BASKETBALL, ZIPPER, SNOWMOBILE, ELECTRIC LIGHTBULB, TELEPHONE

Je parle français

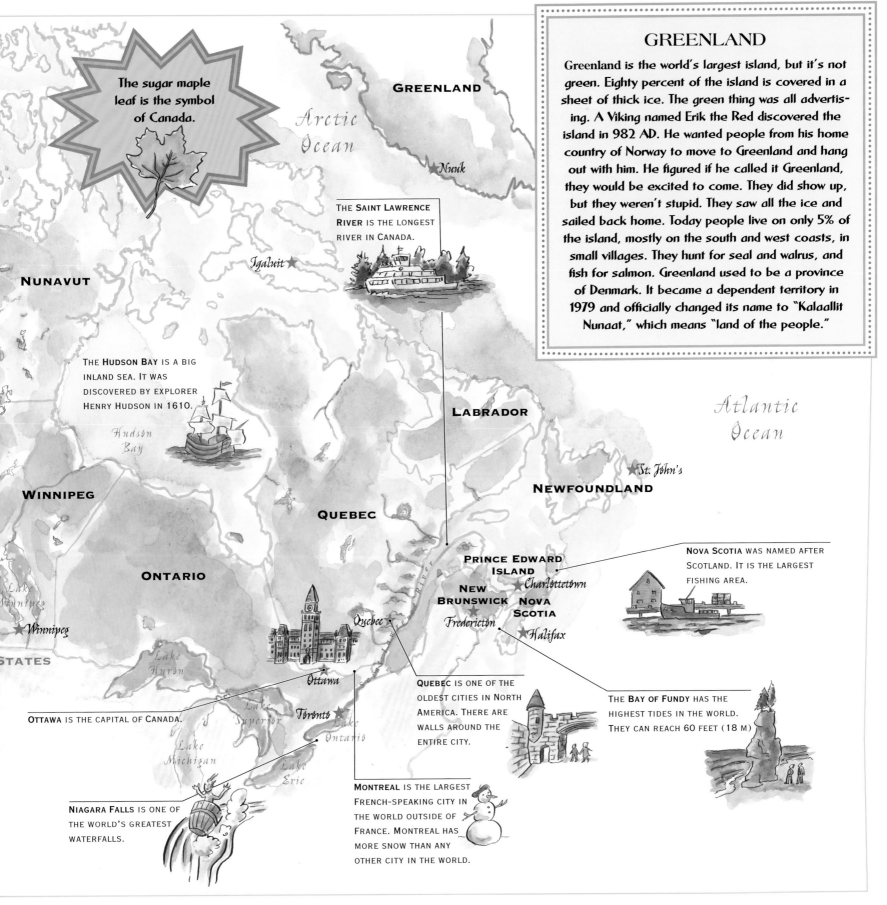

The sugar maple leaf is the symbol of Canada.

GREENLAND

Arctic Ocean

Nuuk

GREENLAND

Greenland is the world's largest island, but it's not green. Eighty percent of the island is covered in a sheet of thick ice. The green thing was all advertising. A Viking named Erik the Red discovered the island in 982 AD. He wanted people from his home country of Norway to move to Greenland and hang out with him. He figured if he called it Greenland, they would be excited to come. They did show up, but they weren't stupid. They saw all the ice and sailed back home. Today people live on only 5% of the island, mostly on the south and west coasts, in small villages. They hunt for seal and walrus, and fish for salmon. Greenland used to be a province of Denmark. It became a dependent territory in 1979 and officially changed its name to "Kalaallit Nunaat," which means "land of the people."

THE SAINT LAWRENCE RIVER IS THE LONGEST RIVER IN CANADA.

NUNAVUT

Iqaluit ★

THE HUDSON BAY IS A BIG INLAND SEA. IT WAS DISCOVERED BY EXPLORER HENRY HUDSON IN 1610.

Hudson Bay

LABRADOR

Atlantic Ocean

St. John's

NEWFOUNDLAND

WINNIPEG

QUEBEC

Lake Winnipeg

★ *Winnipeg*

ONTARIO

PRINCE EDWARD ISLAND

NOVA SCOTIA WAS NAMED AFTER SCOTLAND. IT IS THE LARGEST FISHING AREA.

Charlottetown

NEW BRUNSWICK

NOVA SCOTIA

STATES

Lake Huron

Quebec

Fredericton

Halifax

Lake Superior

Ottawa

Lake Michigan

Toronto

Lake Ontario

Lake Erie

OTTAWA IS THE CAPITAL OF CANADA.

QUEBEC IS ONE OF THE OLDEST CITIES IN NORTH AMERICA. THERE ARE WALLS AROUND THE ENTIRE CITY.

THE BAY OF FUNDY HAS THE HIGHEST TIDES IN THE WORLD. THEY CAN REACH 60 FEET (18 M)

NIAGARA FALLS IS ONE OF THE WORLD'S GREATEST WATERFALLS.

MONTREAL IS THE LARGEST FRENCH-SPEAKING CITY IN THE WORLD OUTSIDE OF FRANCE. MONTREAL HAS MORE SNOW THAN ANY OTHER CITY IN THE WORLD.

Mexico

Mexico is a nation with a rich culture and an amazing landscape. Located directly south of the United States, Mexico is bordered on the west by the Pacific Ocean and on the east by the Gulf of Mexico. Mexico is about three times larger than the state of Texas. It is divided into thirty-one states, plus the Federal District of Mexico City.

Mexico has long stretches of desert, but it also has tropical rainforests, soaring mountains, and some of the most beautiful beaches in the world. The Sierra Madre Mountains run through the center of the country. They are a continuation of the Rocky Mountains from the United States.

The people of Mexico descended from the Aztec and Mayan Native Peoples and the Spanish. Mexico was owned by Spain for over three hundred years, so that's why most people speak Spanish. In fact, Mexico is the largest Spanish-speaking country in the world.

What Is a Hurricane?

A HURRICANE IS A HUGE AND POWERFUL TROPICAL STORM. ITS WINDS CAN REACH OVER 200 MILES (322 KM) PER HOUR. THEY START IN THE OPEN ATLANTIC OCEAN, AND THE WARM WATERS INCREASE THE STORM'S POWER. A HURRICANE ROTATES COUNTERCLOCKWISE (THAT'S THE OPPOSITE WAY THE HANDS GO ON A CLOCK), AND THE CENTER OF THE STORM IS CALLED THE "EYE." FUNNY THING—THE EYE IS THE CALMEST PART OF THE STORM! HURRICANE SEASON IN THE ATLANTIC OCEAN IS FROM JUNE TO NOVEMBER. THE CARIBBEAN IS OFTEN HIT BY HURRICANES, AND THE WINDS AND RAIN CAUSE A LOT OF DAMAGE. THE ISLAND OF GRAND CAYMAN HAS BEEN HIT BY THE MOST HURRICANES— SIXTY-FOUR TIMES SINCE 1871.

SIERRA MADRES

UNITED STATES

Pacific Ocean

MEXICO

SIERRA MADRE MOUNTAINS

Holiday Highlight

ON LA DÍA DE LOS MUERTOS, OR DAY OF THE DEAD, MEXICANS REMEMBER LOVED ONES WHO HAVE DIED. DURING THE FESTIVAL, PEOPLE PRAY THAT THE SOULS OF THEIR RELATIVES RETURN TO EARTH FOR JUST THIS ONE DAY. FAMILIES HAVE PICNIC MEALS IN GRAVEYARDS AND DECORATE THE GRAVESITES WITH CANDY AND MARIGOLD FLOWERS. SKELETONS SCULPTED FROM SUGAR ARE DISPLAYED, AND LOAFS OF BREAD ARE BAKED IN THE SHAPE OF SKELETONS. BELIEVE IT OR NOT, THIS IS A HAPPY HOLIDAY TO CELEBRATE DEAD FAMILY MEMBERS.

MEXICO CITY IS THE CAPITAL AND THE LARGEST CITY IN MEXICO, WITH OVER 19 MILLION PEOPLE.

Mexico City

What You Need to Know about Mexico

MAIN CROPS: CORN, CHILE PEPPER, BEANS, WHEAT, AVOCADO

SOME NATIVE ANIMALS: MEXICAN GRAY WOLF, PUMA, COYOTE, OCELOT

MAIN LANGUAGES: SPANISH

CULTURAL HOLIDAYS: CINCO DE MAYO, DÍA DE LOS MUERTOS (DAY OF THE DEAD), INDEPENDENCE DAY, LAS POSADAS

FAVORITE SPORTS: SOCCER, BULLFIGHTING

FAVORITE FOODS: TACOS, ROASTED CHILES, TORTILLAS

INVENTIONS: CHOCOLATE, COLOR TELEVISION, THE NUMBER ZERO

ACAPULCO AND CANCÚN ARE POPULAR BEACH RESORTS.

TIKAL, GUATEMALA, IS AN ANCIENT MAYAN CITY IN A TROPICAL RAINFOREST.

IN PANAMA YOU CAN SEE THE SUNRISE AND SUNSET FROM THE SAME BEACH.

Central America and The Caribbean

Central America

Central America is a tropical **isthmus**. An isthmus is a narrow piece of land that connects two larger lands the same way a bridge does. Central America connects North America and South America.

Native Americans lived in Central America before the Europeans came over. Spain colonized (that means took control over) Central America, and the main language spoken here is still Spanish.

Central America has seven independent countries. The middle part of the region is covered with volcanoes. The largest river, the Rio Coco, flows through Nicaragua.

Central America is home to many amazing animals and plants. The Bosawás Biosphere Reserve in Nicaragua is the second-largest rainforest after the Amazon in South America, and off the shore of Belize is a magnificent coral reef with brightly colored tropical fish. It's the second-largest coral reef in the world.

The Caribbean

Do you enjoy playing on a sandy beach? Or swimming in warm, turquoise waters? Then the Caribbean Islands are the place for you! There are over seven thousand islands in the Caribbean. The islands are called the West Indies, because when Columbus landed here in 1492, he thought he'd reached the islands off India. The islands separate the calm Caribbean Sea from the Atlantic Ocean, and they boast beautiful sandy beaches and tall palm trees.

Gulf of Mexico

CUBA IS THE LARGEST CARIBBEAN ISLAND. HAVANA IS THE LARGEST CITY.

THE BAHAMAS

Havana
CUBA

JAMAICA IS THE BIRTHPLACE OF REGGAE MUSIC.

CHICHÉN ITZÁ IS AN ANCIENT MAYAN PYRAMID.

SIAN KA'AN BIOSPHERE RESERVE IS A LARGE PROTECTED WETLANDS AREA.

JAMAICA
Kingston

DOMINICAN REPUBLIC

PUERTO RICO

HAITI
Port-au-Prince
Santo Domingo

THE PEOPLE OF HAITI SPEAK FRENCH

BONJOU!

GRENADA IS THE SPICE ISLAND. NUTMEG, CINNAMON, AND CLOVES ARE GROWN HERE.

TRINIDAD IS THE HOME OF CALYPSO MUSIC PLAYED ON STEEL DRUMS.

Belmopan
BELIZE

GUATEMALA
Guatemala City

HONDURAS
Tegucigalpa

BELIZE IS THE ONLY ENGLISH-SPEAKING COUNTRY IN CENTRAL AMERICA.

Caribbean Sea

San Salvador
EL SALVADOR

NICARAGUA
Managua

HABLAMOS INGLÉS!

COSTA RICA
San José

THE PANAMA CANAL ALLOWS SHIPS TO CROSS CENTRAL AMERICA FROM ONE OCEAN INTO THE OTHER. THE CANAL IS MAN-MADE AND CROSSES 50 MILES (80 KM) OVER THE COUNTRY OF PANAMA.

PANAMA
Panama City

SOUTH AMERICA

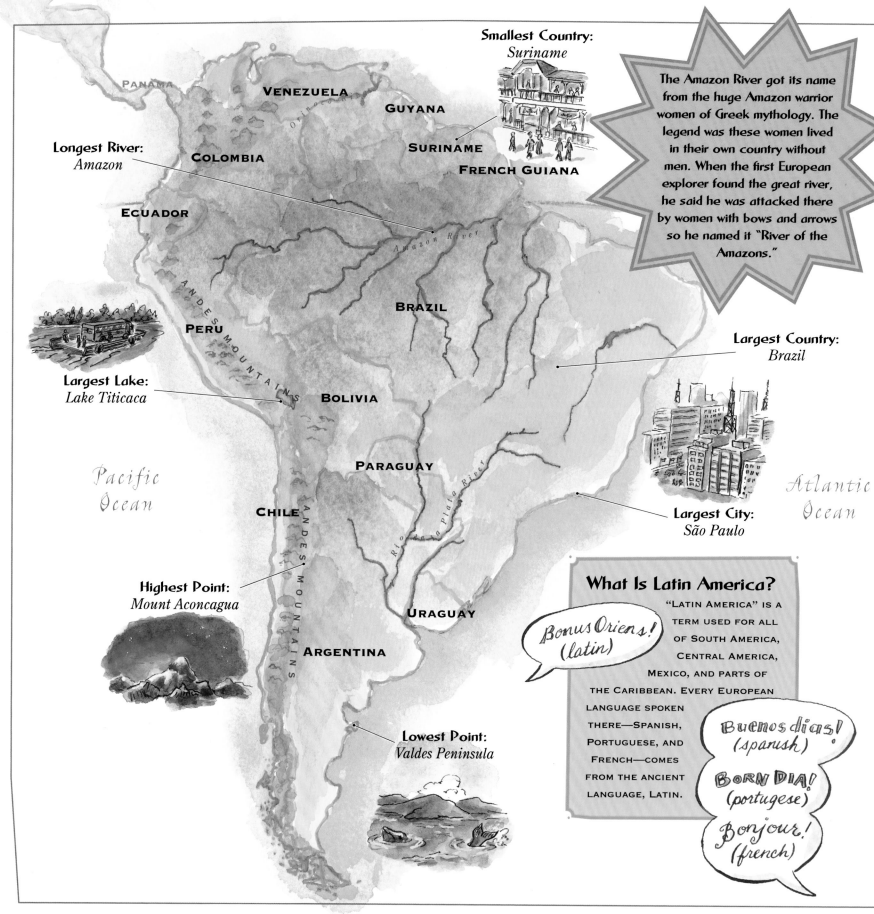

Smallest Country:
Suriname

PANAMA

VENEZUELA

GUYANA

SURINAME

FRENCH GUIANA

The Amazon River got its name from the huge Amazon warrior women of Greek mythology. The legend was these women lived in their own country without men. When the first European explorer found the great river, he said he was attacked there by women with bows and arrows so he named it "River of the Amazons."

Longest River:
Amazon

COLOMBIA

ECUADOR

Amazon River

BRAZIL

PERU

Largest Country:
Brazil

Largest Lake:
Lake Titicaca

BOLIVIA

Pacific Ocean

PARAGUAY

Rio de la Plata River

Largest City:
São Paulo

Atlantic Ocean

CHILE

Highest Point:
Mount Aconcagua

URAGUAY

What Is Latin America?

"LATIN AMERICA" IS A TERM USED FOR ALL OF SOUTH AMERICA, CENTRAL AMERICA, MEXICO, AND PARTS OF THE CARIBBEAN. EVERY EUROPEAN LANGUAGE SPOKEN THERE—SPANISH, PORTUGUESE, AND FRENCH—COMES FROM THE ANCIENT LANGUAGE, LATIN.

Bonus Oriens! (latin)

ARGENTINA

Buenos dias! (spanish)

Born Dia! (portugese)

Lowest Point:
Valdes Peninsula

Bonjour! (french)

South America

When you think South America, think the letter **A**. A is for Andes Mountains and Amazon River. These two forces dominate the South American landscape.

South America is the fourth-largest continent, and it is located mostly in the Southern Hemisphere. It reaches from the equator down to the South Pole. The Atlantic Ocean borders its east coast, the Pacific Ocean borders its west coast, and the Caribbean Sea borders part of its north coast. It is made up of twelve countries, plus France's territory French Guiana.

South America is a continent of tropical rainforests, snow-capped mountains, extremely dry deserts, emerald mines, ruins of ancient civilizations, and modern cities.

The **Andes Mountains** cover 4,500 miles (7,242 km) along the western coast. This is more than four times the distance of the Rocky Mountains and the longest unbroken mountain chain in the world. The Andes Mountains rank second (behind the Himalayas in Asia) in height. The bases of the mountains are in a warm, tropical climate, but the tall peaks are covered in snow.

The **Amazon River** starts in the Andes Mountains in Peru and stretches about 4,000 miles (6,437 km) across South America until it empties into the Atlantic. It carries more water than any other river in the world, and it has more than a thousand tributaries. The Amazon rainforest is the world's largest rainforest (it's bigger than Australia!) and covers much of the northern and middle part of the continent.

Before the Europeans came over, the Inca civilization was the center of activity in South America. The Incas built amazing roads, temples, and fortresses. In the 1500s, Spain and Portugal took control of the continent, and most countries gained independence in the 1800s.

What You Need to Know about South America

MAIN CROPS: BANANAS, CORN, SWEET POTATOES, TOMATOES, BEANS

SOME NATIVE ANIMALS: LLAMA, ALPACA, MACAW, GIANT SNAKES, ANTEATER

MAIN LANGUAGES: SPANISH, EXCEPT FOR BRAZIL, WHERE PORTUGUESE IS SPOKEN

CULTURAL HOLIDAYS: SAN SEBASTIÁN DE YUMBEL, CARNAVAL, DÍA DEL TRABAJADOR (INTERNATIONAL DAY OF THE WORKER)

FAVORITE SPORTS: SOCCER, BOXING, HORSE RACING

FAVORITE FOODS: FEIJOADA, EMPANADA, DULCE DE LECHE, CHURRASCO, SEVICHE

INVENTIONS: LATEX, POPCORN, UMBRELLA, TOOTHBRUSH, MIRRORS

Northern South America and Brazil

The northern part of South America features the Andes Mountains, the Amazon River, and the rainforest. Most people live along the coast. Venezuela is the wealthiest country in this area because of its oil reserves. Brazil takes up nearly half of South America and is the fifth-largest country in the world—larger than the entire continental United States! Over 60% of the Amazon rainforest is in Brazil. Brazil has huge, modern cities, but it also has areas in the rainforest that have never been explored.

Pacific Ocean

COTOPAXI IN ECUADOR IS ONE OF THE TALLEST, ACTIVE VOLCANOES IN THE WORLD.

CHARLES DARWIN AND THE GALÁPAGOS ISLANDS

The Galápagos are an archipelago of nineteen islands in the Pacific Ocean, off the coast of Ecuador. The islands are home to gigantic tortoises (we're talking 500 pounds or 2,270 kg!) who live to be two hundred years old. In 1835, an English scientist named Charles Darwin landed there. While checking out the wildlife, he noticed that each island had finches (small brown birds) that looked almost the same, except for their beaks. Some beaks were short, some were long, some were pointy, and some were rounded. From the Galápagos finches, Darwin came up with the idea of evolution and "natural selection." He said that the finches all descended from one original finch, but over hundreds of years, their appearances changed to allow them to survive the environment of each island. So if one island had only shellfish to eat, the finch's beak gradually became thicker to crack the shells, whereas if one island only had bugs in trees to eat, the finch's beak became skinnier to suck out the bugs.

Eats insects

Eats buds & fruit

Eats leaves

The Lost City of Machu Picchu

MACHU PICCHU IS AN ANCIENT INCA CITY IN THE MOUNTAINS OF PERU. MACHU PICCHU WAS BUILT IN THE 1400S, BUT WHEN THE SPANISH CAME OVER IN THE 1500S AND DESTROYED MANY INCA SETTLEMENTS, THEY SOMEHOW MISSED THIS ONE. OVER THE YEARS, THE JUNGLE GREW ON TOP OF THIS DESERTED TOWN, BURYING IT AND KEEPING IT SECRET. IT WAS REDISCOVERED IN 1911, AND EXPLORERS FOUND OVER TWO HUNDRED STONE BUILDINGS THERE.

Holiday Highlight

BRAZIL'S MOST POPULAR FESTIVAL IS **CARNAVAL**, WHICH HAPPENS RIGHT BEFORE LENT (A FORTY-DAY PERIOD BEFORE EASTER). CARNAVAL IN THE CITY OF RIO DE JANEIRO IS THOUGHT TO BE THE BIGGEST CELEBRATION IN THE WORLD. IT FEATURES THOUSANDS OF PEOPLE IN FANCY, WILD COSTUMES WHO DANCE THROUGH THE STREETS ALONGSIDE DECORATED FLOATS. THERE ARE ALSO HUGE PARTIES AND SAMBA COMPETITIONS.

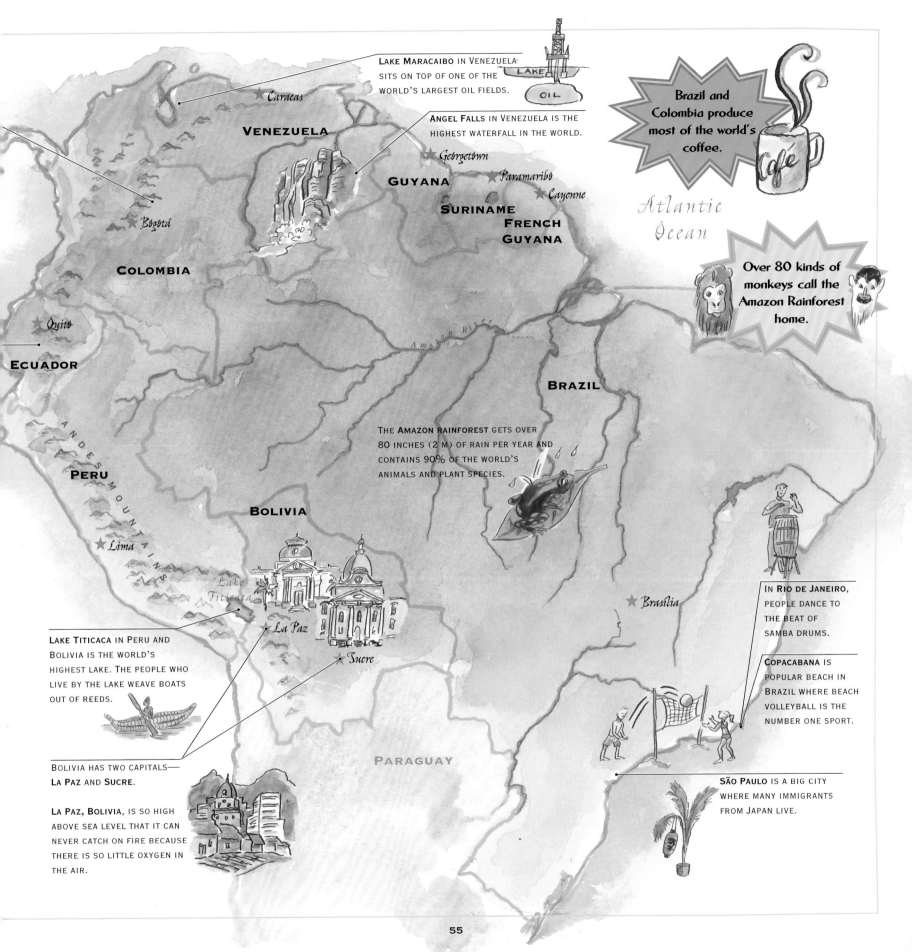

LAKE MARACAIBO IN VENEZUELA SITS ON TOP OF ONE OF THE WORLD'S LARGEST OIL FIELDS.

ANGEL FALLS IN VENEZUELA IS THE HIGHEST WATERFALL IN THE WORLD.

★ Caracas

VENEZUELA

★ Georgetown

GUYANA

★ Paramaribo

★ Cayenne

SURINAME

FRENCH GUYANA

Brazil and Colombia produce most of the world's coffee.

café

Atlantic Ocean

COLOMBIA

★ Bogotá

Over 80 kinds of monkeys call the Amazon Rainforest home.

Amazon River

ECUADOR

★ Quito

BRAZIL

THE AMAZON RAINFOREST GETS OVER 80 INCHES (2 M) OF RAIN PER YEAR AND CONTAINS 90% OF THE WORLD'S ANIMALS AND PLANT SPECIES.

PERU

★ Lima

ANDES MOUNTAINS

BOLIVIA

Lake Titicaca

★ La Paz

★ Sucre

★ Brasília

IN RIO DE JANEIRO, PEOPLE DANCE TO THE BEAT OF SAMBA DRUMS.

LAKE TITICACA IN PERU AND BOLIVIA IS THE WORLD'S HIGHEST LAKE. THE PEOPLE WHO LIVE BY THE LAKE WEAVE BOATS OUT OF REEDS.

COPACABANA IS POPULAR BEACH IN BRAZIL WHERE BEACH VOLLEYBALL IS THE NUMBER ONE SPORT.

BOLIVIA HAS TWO CAPITALS— LA PAZ AND SUCRE.

PARAGUAY

SÃO PAULO IS A BIG CITY WHERE MANY IMMIGRANTS FROM JAPAN LIVE.

LA PAZ, BOLIVIA, IS SO HIGH ABOVE SEA LEVEL THAT IT CAN NEVER CATCH ON FIRE BECAUSE THERE IS SO LITTLE OXYGEN IN THE AIR.

ATACAMA DESERT IN NORTHERN CHILE IS THE DRIEST PLACE ON EARTH. SOME PARTS HAVE NEVER GOTTEN A DROP OF RAIN!

PARAGUAY

BRAZIL

Asunción

Rio de la Plata River

IGUAZU FALLS IS ONE OF THE WORLD'S WIDEST WATERFALLS.

1.67 miles

CHILE

ACONCAGUA IN THE ANDES MOUNTAINS IN PERU IS THE HIGHEST MOUNTAIN IN THE WESTERN HEMISPHERE.

Santiago

URUGUAY

Montevideo

Buenos Aires

ANDES MOUNTAINS

ARGENTINA

BUENOS AIRES, ARGENTINA, IS THE HOME OF THE TANGO DANCE.

Atlantic Ocean

Pacific Ocean

PUNTA ARENAS IS THE WORLD'S SOUTHERNMOST CITY.

SOUTH AMERICA

Drake Passage

ANTARCTICA

DRAKE PASSAGE SEPARATES SOUTH AMERICA FROM ANTARCTICA.

THE AWESOME MORENO GLACIER IS ON THE SOUTHERNMOST TIP OF ARGENTINA.

CAPE HORN ISLAND IS THE SOUTHERNMOST SPOT IN SOUTH AMERICA. BEFORE THE PANAMA CANAL WAS BUILT, SAILORS HAD TO NAVIGATE ITS ROUGH WATERS TO GET FROM THE ATLANTIC OCEAN TO THE PACIFIC OCEAN.

The only place the Atlantic and Pacific Oceans meet is at the tip of South America.

National Poncho Festival

THE CITY OF SAN FERNANDO DEL VALLE DE CATAMARCA IN NORTHWEST ARGENTINA IS HOME TO THE FAMOUS NATIONAL PONCHO FESTIVAL (FIESTA NACIONAL DEL PONCHO). EVERY JULY, WHICH IS WINTER IN THIS SOUTHERN HEMISPHERE CONTINENT, WEAVERS FROM ALL OVER THE COUNTRY DISPLAY AND SELL DECORATED, WOVEN PONCHOS. **PONCHOS** ARE BLANKET-LIKE CLOAKS WITH A HOLE IN THE CENTER FOR YOUR HEAD. THE WOOL FOR THE PONCHOS COMES FROM LLAMAS, ALPACAS, AND SHEEP.

ISLAND OF MYSTERY

Easter Island is a strange place. The island of volcanic rock, in the middle of the Pacific Ocean, is about 2,200 miles off the coast of Chile, making it most isolated place on Earth. It was called Rapa Nui, until a Dutch sea captain landed there on Easter Sunday in 1722, and renamed it Easter Island. But that's not the strange part. Easter Island is best known for its GIANT face-like stone statues, called "moai," that line its coastline, as if guarding the island from invaders. Each statue is about fourteen feet tall and weighs about fourteen tons. Now that's strange! What's even stranger is that no one can explain why the people who lived there long ago carved 887 enormous statues and how they managed to move them around the island. Some people believe the statues represented the spirits of their chieftans and gods.

All the countries in the southern part of South America were once Spanish colonies, and the Spanish influence is still strong there. The landscape is all about extremes—the extreme height of the mountains, the extreme temperatures (tropical Paraguay to the glaciers of Argentina), and the extreme **pampas**. The pampas is a large grassland that covers Uruguay and Argentina. Herds of cattle are bred there. Top restaurants around the world serve delicious beef from this region. **Gauchos** work on ranches on the pampas of Argentina, herding the cattle with a lasso or a *boleadoras*—three hard leather balls attached to a rope. A gaucho is like the American cowboy.

In Patagonia, a desert in southern Argentina, sheep are raised for their fabulous wool. Even though Patagonia is a desert, it's not hot. It's just really dry. The Andes Mountains act like a wall, holding back all the moisture from the Pacific Ocean and all the rivers and streams. This makes the west side of the country wet and the east side dry.

Europe

Europe is the second-smallest continent, but it's the most crowded. It comprises forty-six countries and they're all packed with people who live mostly in urban cities and towns.

Europe is in the northern hemisphere and is bordered by the Atlantic Ocean, the Arctic Ocean, the Norwegian Sea, the Baltic Sea, and the Mediterranean Sea. All that water gives it a very ragged coastline with many bays and peninsulas. The towering Alps Mountains stretch across the continent. There are large forests in the northern areas by the Arctic Circle and gorgeous beaches in the southern areas along the Mediterranean Sea. Europe is the only continent that does not have a desert.

Europe is attached to Asia, and sometimes the two together are called "Eurasia." The border between the two continents goes along the Ural Mountains, the Ural River, and the Caspian Sea. It slices through the countries of Russia and Turkey, so these two countries are actually in two continents! However, in this book we have placed Russia and Turkey with Asia (you can look for them later).

Scientists think people first came to Europe about thirty-six thousand years ago. Europe is often called the birthplace of Western civilization because it was here that major discoveries and developments in science, technology, the arts, and, of course, geography occurred. Today there are many different cultures in this small continent. More than fifty different languages are spoken in Europe, and most Europeans speak more than one language.

What Is the Euro?

EUROPE HAS SO MANY COUNTRIES, MANY OF THEM SMALL, AND PEOPLE EASILY GO BACK AND FORTH BETWEEN THEM. FOR CENTURIES, EVERY COUNTRY HAD ITS OWN MONEY, SO EVERY TIME PEOPLE WANTED TO BUY SOMETHING IN THE COUNTRY NEXT DOOR, EVEN THE LITTLEST THING LIKE A STICK OF GUM, THEY HAD TO EXCHANGE THEIR MONEY TO GET THE BILLS AND COINS OF THE COUNTRY THEY WERE VISITING. EXCHANGING MONEY WAS A PAIN—AND IT COST MONEY, TOO. IN 2002, MANY EUROPEAN COUNTRIES BANDED TOGETHER AND CREATED ONE CURRENCY TO BE SHARED. IT IS CALLED THE **EURO.**

hej! (swedish)
hello! (english)
Heior Buorre beaivvi! (sami)

приbet! (Bulgarian)
ЗАРАВО! (Macedonian)

bonjour! (french)
Alo! (breton)

sveiki! (latvian)
laba diena! (lithuanian)

tere! (estonian)
привіт! (ukranian)

Arctic Ocean

NORTHERN EUROPE

Norwegian Sea

RUSSIA

Largest Lake:
Lake Vanern

UNITED KINGDOM & IRELAND

Lowest Point One:
Lemmefjord

Lowest Point Two:
Prins Alexander Polder

Baltic Sea

Largest Country:
Ukraine

Biggest City:
London

EASTERN EUROPE

Atlantic Ocean

WESTERN EUROPE

Highest Point:
Mont Blanc

Longest River:
Danube

Smallest Country:
Vatican City

SOUTHERN EUROPE

Mediterranean Sea

THE MIDDLE EAST

AFRICA

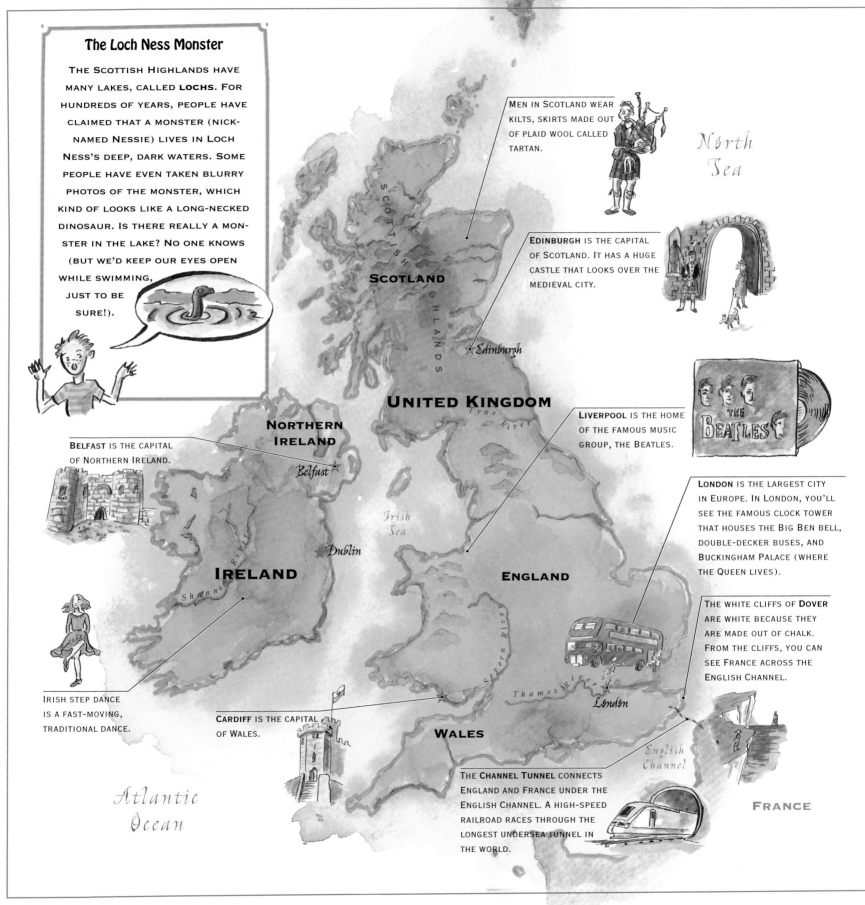

The Loch Ness Monster

THE SCOTTISH HIGHLANDS HAVE MANY LAKES, CALLED **LOCHS**. FOR HUNDREDS OF YEARS, PEOPLE HAVE CLAIMED THAT A MONSTER (NICK-NAMED NESSIE) LIVES IN LOCH NESS'S DEEP, DARK WATERS. SOME PEOPLE HAVE EVEN TAKEN BLURRY PHOTOS OF THE MONSTER, WHICH KIND OF LOOKS LIKE A LONG-NECKED DINOSAUR. IS THERE REALLY A MON-STER IN THE LAKE? NO ONE KNOWS (BUT WE'D KEEP OUR EYES OPEN WHILE SWIMMING, JUST TO BE SURE!).

MEN IN SCOTLAND WEAR KILTS, SKIRTS MADE OUT OF PLAID WOOL CALLED TARTAN.

North Sea

EDINBURGH IS THE CAPITAL OF SCOTLAND. IT HAS A HUGE CASTLE THAT LOOKS OVER THE MEDIEVAL CITY.

SCOTLAND

SCOTTISH HIGHLANDS

Edinburgh

UNITED KINGDOM

Tyne River

LIVERPOOL IS THE HOME OF THE FAMOUS MUSIC GROUP, THE BEATLES.

THE BEATLES

NORTHERN IRELAND

BELFAST IS THE CAPITAL OF NORTHERN IRELAND.

Belfast

Irish Sea

Dublin

IRELAND

Shannon River

ENGLAND

LONDON IS THE LARGEST CITY IN EUROPE. IN LONDON, YOU'LL SEE THE FAMOUS CLOCK TOWER THAT HOUSES THE BIG BEN BELL, DOUBLE-DECKER BUSES, AND BUCKINGHAM PALACE (WHERE THE QUEEN LIVES).

Severn River

THE WHITE CLIFFS OF **DOVER** ARE WHITE BECAUSE THEY ARE MADE OUT OF CHALK. FROM THE CLIFFS, YOU CAN SEE FRANCE ACROSS THE ENGLISH CHANNEL.

Thames River

London

IRISH STEP DANCE IS A FAST-MOVING, TRADITIONAL DANCE.

CARDIFF IS THE CAPITAL OF WALES.

WALES

English Channel

THE **CHANNEL TUNNEL** CONNECTS ENGLAND AND FRANCE UNDER THE ENGLISH CHANNEL. A HIGH-SPEED RAILROAD RACES THROUGH THE LONGEST UNDERSEA TUNNEL IN THE WORLD.

Atlantic Ocean

FRANCE

The United Kingdom and Ireland

Okay, there's a lot to keep straight in this part of Europe.

#1: The United Kingdom (also called the UK) is one country that contains four different areas or smaller countries (England, Scotland, Wales, and Northern Ireland).

#2: The United Kingdom has two sections: Great Britain (England, Scotland, Wales) and Northern Ireland. The Irish Sea divides Northern Ireland from Great Britain.

#3: Ireland is a totally separate country from the United Kingdom. But Northern Ireland is part of the United Kingdom. Kind of confusing? Basically, this has to do with people of two religions (Catholics and Protestants) who were unable to get along, so they divided the country into two.

Holiday Highlight

ON **MAY DAY** (MAY 1), CHILDREN IN ENGLAND'S COUNTRYSIDE DANCE AROUND TALL POLES DECORATED WITH RIBBONS—CALLED **MAYPOLES**—TO CELEBRATE THE RETURN OF SPRING. AS THE CHILDREN DANCE, THE COLORFUL RIBBONS WEAVE TOGETHER AROUND THE POLE. GIRLS DECORATE HOOPS WITH FLOWERS AND MAKE FLOWER GARLANDS FOR THEIR HAIR.

What You Need to Know about the United Kingdom and Ireland

MAIN CROPS: POTATOES, WHEAT, BARLEY, OATS, SUGAR BEET

SOME NATIVE ANIMALS: DEER, FOX, HEDGEHOG

MAIN LANGUAGES: ENGLISH, GAELIC, WELSH

CULTURAL HOLIDAYS: MAY DAY, SAINT PATRICK'S DAY, BOXING DAY, QUEEN'S BIRTHDAY, GUY FAWKES DAY

FAVORITE SPORTS: CRICKET, RUGBY, GOLF

FAVORITE FOODS: SHEPHERD'S PIE, SHORTBREAD, FISH AND CHIPS

INVENTIONS: JET ENGINE, PENICILLIN, RUBBER BAND, LAWN MOWER, TOILET PAPER

PEOPLE DRIVE CARS ON THE LEFT SIDE OF THE ROAD HERE.

#4: Never (and we mean *never*) call someone from Scotland, Wales, or Northern Ireland "English." The correct word is "British." Someone is only "English" if he or she is from England.

Great Britain and Ireland/Northern Ireland are islands in the northwest corner of Europe, floating in the chilly waters of the Atlantic Ocean. The islands are separated from France by the English Channel and from Norway by the North Sea. The United Kingdom is one of the most powerful nations in the world and most of its people live in cities. It has jagged coastlines surrounding high mountains in the north and rolling, green farmland in the south. Ireland, a much more rural country, is called "the Emerald Isle" because of its lush, green fields. The climate is mild in both places but always very, very rainy.

The five Nordic countries—Denmark, Norway, Sweden, Finland, and Iceland—are in the northernmost part of Europe. These countries are also called **Scandinavia** (although really that only means Denmark, Norway, and Sweden). Surrounded by the seas, these countries are peninsulas, except for Iceland, which is an island.

The land is covered with dark pine forests and deep lakes. There are spiky glacier mountains in Norway and Sweden, but the rest of the area is flat countryside. Many of Norway's mountain ranges are broken up by **fjords**. A fjord is a deep, narrow inlet from the sea with high, steep cliff walls. Fjords are caused by glacier erosion.

Throughout the Nordic area, you will find Viking ruins (this area was settled by the Vikings a thousand years ago), medieval castles, and hot spring geysers. The climate is icy cold in the winter but come summer, it is warm and sunny. Even Iceland gets warm! The island has natural hot springs that warm the island and its waters.

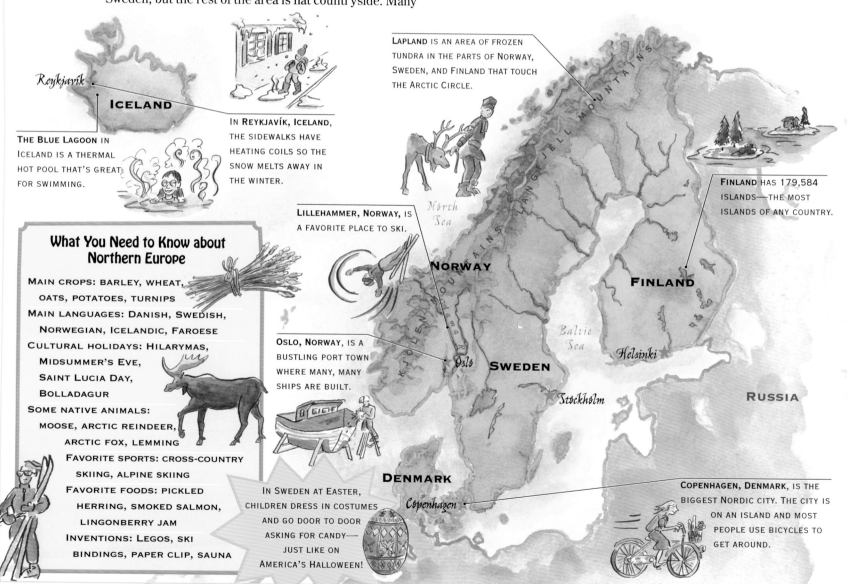

LAPLAND IS AN AREA OF FROZEN TUNDRA IN THE PARTS OF NORWAY, SWEDEN, AND FINLAND THAT TOUCH THE ARCTIC CIRCLE.

ICELAND

Reykjavík

THE **BLUE LAGOON** IN ICELAND IS A THERMAL HOT POOL THAT'S GREAT FOR SWIMMING.

IN **REYKJAVÍK, ICELAND,** THE SIDEWALKS HAVE HEATING COILS SO THE SNOW MELTS AWAY IN THE WINTER.

FINLAND HAS 179,584 ISLANDS—THE MOST ISLANDS OF ANY COUNTRY.

LILLEHAMMER, NORWAY, IS A FAVORITE PLACE TO SKI.

North Sea

NORWAY

FINLAND

What You Need to Know about Northern Europe

MAIN CROPS: BARLEY, WHEAT, OATS, POTATOES, TURNIPS

MAIN LANGUAGES: DANISH, SWEDISH, NORWEGIAN, ICELANDIC, FAROESE

CULTURAL HOLIDAYS: HILARYMAS, MIDSUMMER'S EVE, SAINT LUCIA DAY, BOLLADAGUR

SOME NATIVE ANIMALS: MOOSE, ARCTIC REINDEER, ARCTIC FOX, LEMMING

FAVORITE SPORTS: CROSS-COUNTRY SKIING, ALPINE SKIING

FAVORITE FOODS: PICKLED HERRING, SMOKED SALMON, LINGONBERRY JAM

INVENTIONS: LEGOS, SKI BINDINGS, PAPER CLIP, SAUNA

OSLO, NORWAY, IS A BUSTLING PORT TOWN WHERE MANY, MANY SHIPS ARE BUILT.

Oslo

SWEDEN

Baltic Sea

Helsinki

Stockholm

RUSSIA

DENMARK

Copenhagen

IN SWEDEN AT EASTER, CHILDREN DRESS IN COSTUMES AND GO DOOR TO DOOR ASKING FOR CANDY— JUST LIKE ON AMERICA'S HALLOWEEN!

COPENHAGEN, DENMARK, IS THE BIGGEST NORDIC CITY. THE CITY IS ON AN ISLAND AND MOST PEOPLE USE BICYCLES TO GET AROUND.

Eastern Europe

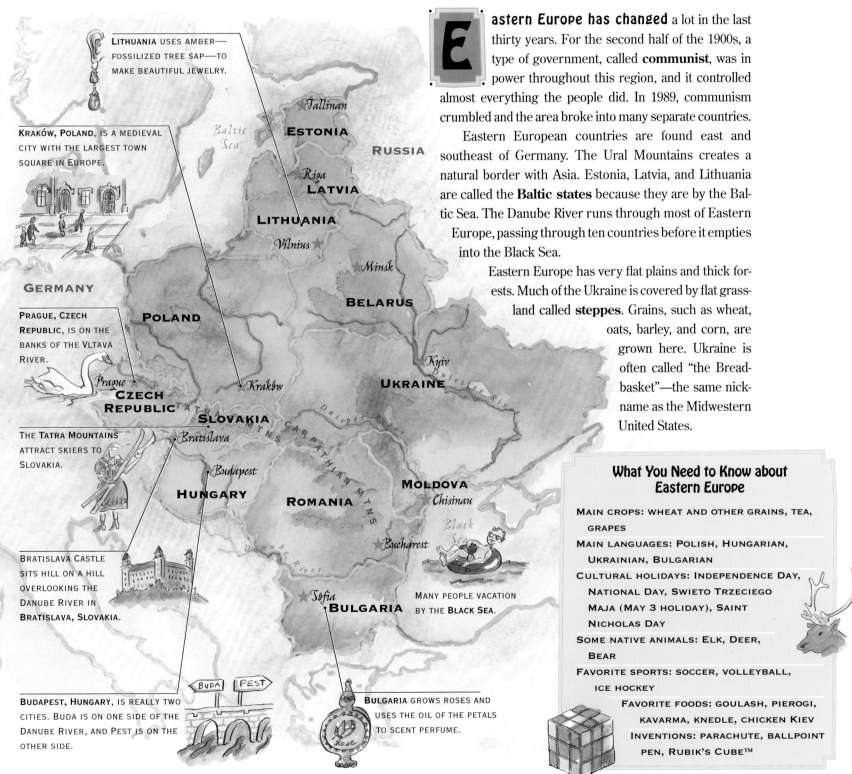

Eastern Europe has changed a lot in the last thirty years. For the second half of the 1900s, a type of government, called **communist**, was in power throughout this region, and it controlled almost everything the people did. In 1989, communism crumbled and the area broke into many separate countries.

Eastern European countries are found east and southeast of Germany. The Ural Mountains creates a natural border with Asia. Estonia, Latvia, and Lithuania are called the **Baltic states** because they are by the Baltic Sea. The Danube River runs through most of Eastern Europe, passing through ten countries before it empties into the Black Sea.

Eastern Europe has very flat plains and thick forests. Much of the Ukraine is covered by flat grassland called **steppes**. Grains, such as wheat, oats, barley, and corn, are grown here. Ukraine is often called "the Breadbasket"—the same nickname as the Midwestern United States.

LITHUANIA USES AMBER—FOSSILIZED TREE SAP—TO MAKE BEAUTIFUL JEWELRY.

KRAKÓW, POLAND, IS A MEDIEVAL CITY WITH THE LARGEST TOWN SQUARE IN EUROPE.

PRAGUE, CZECH REPUBLIC, IS ON THE BANKS OF THE VLTAVA RIVER.

THE TATRA MOUNTAINS ATTRACT SKIERS TO SLOVAKIA.

BRATISLAVA CASTLE SITS HILL ON A HILL OVERLOOKING THE DANUBE RIVER IN BRATISLAVA, SLOVAKIA.

BUDAPEST, HUNGARY, IS REALLY TWO CITIES. BUDA IS ON ONE SIDE OF THE DANUBE RIVER, AND PEST IS ON THE OTHER SIDE.

BULGARIA GROWS ROSES AND USES THE OIL OF THE PETALS TO SCENT PERFUME.

MANY PEOPLE VACATION BY THE BLACK SEA.

What You Need to Know about Eastern Europe

MAIN CROPS: WHEAT AND OTHER GRAINS, TEA, GRAPES

MAIN LANGUAGES: POLISH, HUNGARIAN, UKRAINIAN, BULGARIAN

CULTURAL HOLIDAYS: INDEPENDENCE DAY, NATIONAL DAY, SWIETO TRZECIEGO MAJA (MAY 3 HOLIDAY), SAINT NICHOLAS DAY

SOME NATIVE ANIMALS: ELK, DEER, BEAR

FAVORITE SPORTS: SOCCER, VOLLEYBALL, ICE HOCKEY

FAVORITE FOODS: GOULASH, PIEROGI, KAVARMA, KNEDLE, CHICKEN KIEV

INVENTIONS: PARACHUTE, BALLPOINT PEN, RUBIK'S CUBE™

Western Europe

Western Europe is often called "the heart of Europe." There is so much going on here—mountains that touch the sky, sunny beaches, film festivals, art museums, fairy-tale castles, charming villages, rolling green hills, and lots of delicious foods.

Belgium, the Netherlands, and Luxembourg are called the **Low Countries**, because so much of their flat land lies below sea level. They also share the nickname **Benelux**. (Did you get that it's made up of the first few letters of each country's name?) France is the largest country in Western Europe and is known for its high fashion, enormous country castles called chateaux, and wine-making vineyards. Germany is the most industrialized country, producing cars, machinery, and beer. Austria and Switzerland are covered by the Alps Mountains and lots of forest.

What You Need to Know about Western Europe

MAIN CROPS: ONIONS, GRAPES, POTATOES, BRUSSELS SPROUTS

MAIN LANGUAGES: FRENCH, GERMAN, DUTCH

CULTURAL HOLIDAYS: BASTILLE DAY, GERMAN UNITY DAY, SWISS NATIONAL DAY, QUEEN'S DAY, OCTOBERFEST, TWELFTH NIGHT

SOME NATIVE ANIMALS: RED SQUIRREL, WILD BOAR, FOX, WOLF, DEER, IBEX

FAVORITE SPORTS: SOCCER, FIELD HOCKEY, HANDBALL, CYCLING

FAVORITE FOODS: CREPES, SCHNITZEL, FONDUE, BRATWURST, PRETZELS

INVENTIONS: BICYCLE, HOT AIR BALLOON, PENCIL, CONTACT LENS

Holiday Highlight

CHRISTMAS IS A CHRISTIAN FESTIVAL ON DECEMBER 25, CELEBRATING THE BIRTH OF JESUS CHRIST. ONE OF THE MANY SYMBOLS OF THE HOLIDAY, A DECORATED EVERGREEN TREE, STARTED IN GERMANY. FAMILIES IN MANY COUNTRIES DECORATE THEIR TREES TOGETHER, BUT GERMAN PARENTS DECORATE THEIR TREE SECRETLY AND SURPRISE THEIR CHILDREN WITH IT. ON CHRISTMAS, CHILDREN SING SONGS, CALLED CAROLS, AND GET GIFTS. THEY ALSO MAKE TINY HOUSES OUT OF GINGERBREAD AND SHARE A BIG MEAL WITH THEIR FAMILIES.

DOUBLE-DUTCH JUMP ROPE, WHEN TWO ROPES SWING IN OPPOSITE DIRECTIONS AND CHILDREN JUMP BOTH ROPES AT THE SAME TIME, WAS INVENTED IN THE NETHERLANDS.

Yodel Me!

"CALL ME." "TEXT ME." "YODEL ME." WAIT—DO YOU MEAN YOU'VE NEVER ASKED YOUR FRIEND TO YODEL YOU? WELL, YOU MUST NOT LIVE IN THE SWISS OR AUSTRIAN ALPS. YEARS AGO, PEOPLE IN THE ALPS OFTEN HAD FRIENDS WHO LIVED A MOUNTAIN PEAK OR TWO AWAY. WHEN THEY WANTED TO SAY HI OR SEE IF SOMEONE WANTED TO COME OVER, THEY WOULD YODEL. A YODEL IS A MELODIC, WORDLESS YELL THAT ECHOES THROUGH THE MOUNTAIN RANGE. IT SOUNDS A BIT LIKE "YODEL-AY-EE-OOO." DIFFERENT YODELS HAD DIFFERENT MEANINGS. TODAY YODELING IS A PART OF EUROPEAN FOLK MUSIC.

YODEL ay EE ooo!

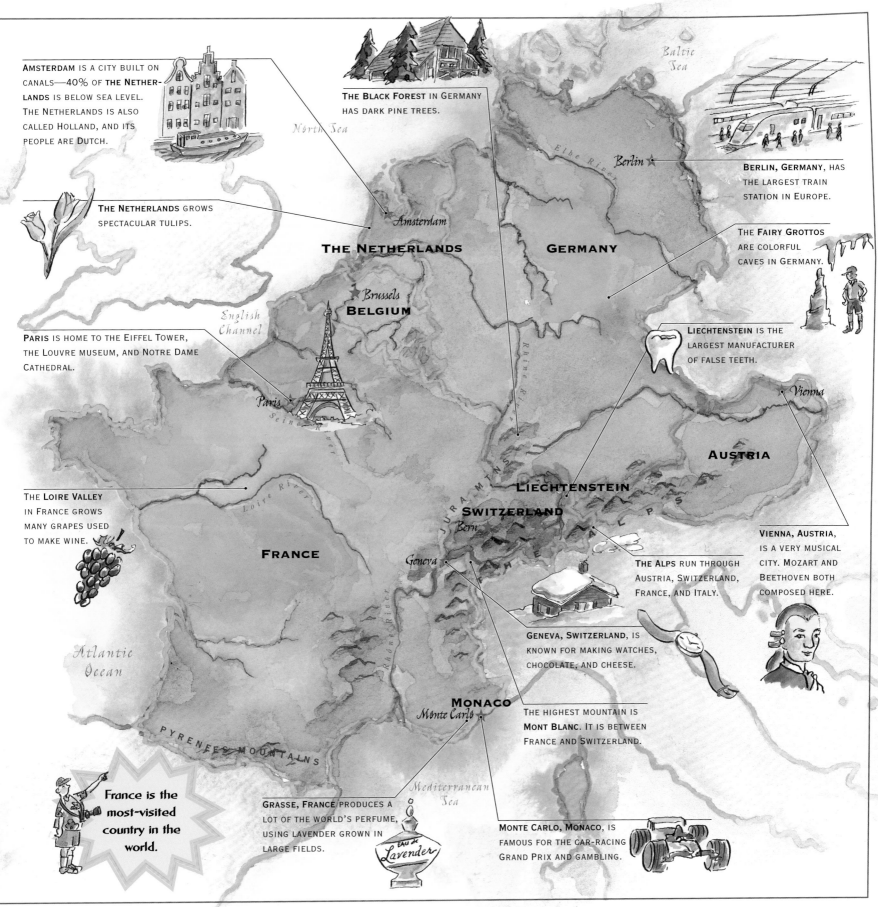

AMSTERDAM IS A CITY BUILT ON CANALS—40% OF THE NETHERLANDS IS BELOW SEA LEVEL. THE NETHERLANDS IS ALSO CALLED HOLLAND, AND ITS PEOPLE ARE DUTCH.

THE BLACK FOREST IN GERMANY HAS DARK PINE TREES.

BERLIN, GERMANY, HAS THE LARGEST TRAIN STATION IN EUROPE.

THE NETHERLANDS GROWS SPECTACULAR TULIPS.

THE FAIRY GROTTOS ARE COLORFUL CAVES IN GERMANY.

LIECHTENSTEIN IS THE LARGEST MANUFACTURER OF FALSE TEETH.

PARIS IS HOME TO THE EIFFEL TOWER, THE LOUVRE MUSEUM, AND NOTRE DAME CATHEDRAL.

THE LOIRE VALLEY IN FRANCE GROWS MANY GRAPES USED TO MAKE WINE.

VIENNA, AUSTRIA, IS A VERY MUSICAL CITY. MOZART AND BEETHOVEN BOTH COMPOSED HERE.

THE ALPS RUN THROUGH AUSTRIA, SWITZERLAND, FRANCE, AND ITALY.

GENEVA, SWITZERLAND, IS KNOWN FOR MAKING WATCHES, CHOCOLATE, AND CHEESE.

THE HIGHEST MOUNTAIN IS MONT BLANC. IT IS BETWEEN FRANCE AND SWITZERLAND.

France is the most-visited country in the world.

GRASSE, FRANCE PRODUCES A LOT OF THE WORLD'S PERFUME, USING LAVENDER GROWN IN LARGE FIELDS.

MONTE CARLO, MONACO, IS FAMOUS FOR THE CAR-RACING GRAND PRIX AND GAMBLING.

Baltic Sea

North Sea

Berlin

Elbe River

Amsterdam

THE NETHERLANDS

GERMANY

Brussels

BELGIUM

English Channel

Rhine River

Vienna

Paris

Seine River

AUSTRIA

LIECHTENSTEIN

JURA MTNS.

SWITZERLAND

Bern

Loire River

FRANCE

Geneva

Rhône River

THE ALPS

Atlantic Ocean

MONACO

Monte Carlo

PYRENEES MOUNTAINS

Mediterranean Sea

EAU de Lavender

What You Need to Know about Southern Europe

MAIN CROPS: GRAPES, OLIVES, DATES, NUTS, FIGS, CITRUS FRUITS

SOME NATIVE ANIMALS: IBEX, BROWN BEAR, SHEEP

MAIN LANGUAGES: SPANISH, PORTUGUESE, ITALIAN, GREEK

CULTURAL HOLIDAYS: FEAST OF SAINT BASIL, APOKRIAS (CARNIVAL SEASON), EPIPHANY (THREE KINGS DAY), GREEK INDEPENDENCE DAY, SAINT GEORGE'S DAY

FAVORITE SPORTS: SOCCER, BASKETBALL, BULLFIGHTING, CYCLING

FAVORITE FOODS: PASTA, RISOTTO, GYRO, CALAMARI, PAELLA, CHORIZO

INVENTIONS: MOP, BATTERY, PIANO, ICE-CREAM CONE, ZAMBONI, COIN MONEY

Italians eat 55 lbs (25 kg) of pasta per person each year.

VENICE, ITALY, HAS CANALS INSTEAD OF STREETS, AND PEOPLE GET AROUND BY BOATS CALLED GONDOLAS INSTEAD OF CARS.

Atlantic Ocean

MADRID IS LOCATED IN THE EXACT CENTER OF SPAIN.

SEVILLE, SPAIN, IS THE BULLFIGHTING CAPITAL OF THE WORLD.

FRANCE

SLOVENIA
Ljubljana

THE LEANING TOWER OF PISA IS A FAMOUS TOWER THAT REALLY IS CROOKED.

CROATIA
Zagreb
Sava River

The Alps
Po River
Adige River

SAN MARINO
San Marino

BOSNIA AND HERZEGOVINA
Sarajevo

Belgrad

PORTUGAL

SPAIN

ANDORRA
Andorra la Vella

ITALY

Adriatic Sea

SERBI

Tagus River

Madrid

Lisbon

Mediterranean Sea

VATICAN CITY
Rome

PENNINES MTNS

MONTENEGRO
Podgorica

Skop

Tiranë

ALBANIA

VATICAN CITY IS THE SMALLEST COUNTRY IN THE WORLD. IT IS INSIDE ROME (THE CAPITAL OF ITALY), AND IT'S WHERE THE POPE LIVES.

NAPLES, ITALY, IS WHERE PIZZA WAS INVENTED TWO HUNDRED YEARS AGO.

Ionian Sea

Portugal is the largest producer of cork. Cork—the stuff used on bulletin boards and as stoppers in wine bottles—comes from the bark of the cork tree. Once the bark is striped off, it takes nine years to grow back.

TUNISIA

DUBROVNIK, CROATIA, IS A CITY SURROUNDED BY HIGH WALLS.

MALTA
Valletta ★

Southern Europe

Don't tell southern Europe not to point fingers, because this area is all about peninsulas. Three major peninsulas jut into the oceans and seas.

#1: The Iberian Peninsula. On the southwestern side, it reaches into the Atlantic Ocean and the Mediterranean Sea and is home to Spain, Portugal, and tiny Andorra. It is only 5 miles (8 km) away from Africa. These three countries are separated from the rest of Europe by the Pyrenees Mountains.

#2: The Italian Peninsula. This boot-shaped peninsula is surrounded by the Mediterranean Sea, the Ionian Sea, and the Adriatic Sea. It is home to the countries of Italy, Vatican City, San Moreno, and the island of Malta.

#3: The Balkan Peninsula. On the southeastern side, it is bordered by the Black Sea, the Aegean Sea, the Mediterranean Sea, the Adriatic Sea, and the Ionian Sea. It contains what are often called the Balkan states (not to be confused with the Baltic states!), which are the countries of: Slovenia, Croatia, Serbia and Montenegro, Bosnia and Herzegovina, Macedonia, Albania, Greece, and Cyprus.

All these peninsulas share a Mediterranean climate—hot, dry summers and mild, rainy winters. The climate here is very much like Southern California. The landscape is mostly dry hills, forests, and plains, except for the northern parts of the area which are covered by the snowy Alps.

This area has civilizations that go back thousands of years. Greece is known as "the birthplace of Western civilization," and Italy was the home of the Roman Empire. Both countries contributed greatly to architecture, art, government, and science, and both have famous ruins —the Colosseum, a stadium in Rome where gladiators fought to their deaths, and the Parthenon in Athens, an ancient temple built to honor the Greek god Athena.

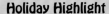

Holiday Highlight

IN GREECE, THE FEAST OF SAINT BASIL IS CELEBRATED ON JANUARY 1. CHILDREN EAT VASILOPITA (VAHS-EEL-OH-PEE-TAH), OR SAINT BASIL'S CAKE. A COIN IS BAKED INTO THE CAKE, AND THE CHILD WHO FINDS THE COIN IS SAID TO HAVE GOOD LUCK FOR THE COMING YEAR.

ROMANIA

Black Sea

T N S

OSOVO

ristina

KOSOVO IS THE NEWEST COUNTRY. IT DECLARED ITS INDEPENDENCE FROM SERBIA IN 2008.

ACEDONIA

DOPE MTNS

TURKEY

REECE

ATHENS, GREECE, IS FAMOUS FOR THE ACROPOLIS AND THE PARTHENON.

Athens

Aegean Sea

Nicosia
CYPRUS

THE GREEK ISLANDS, WITH THEIR BRIGHT WHITE BUILDINGS AND BLUE WATER, ARE POPULAR VACATION SPOTS.

A MARATHON—A RUNNING RACE OF 26 MILES, 385 YARDS (42.2 KM)—IS NAMED AFTER AN ANCIENT GREEK SOLDIER WHO SPRINTED FROM SPARTA TO ATHENS WITHOUT STOPPING, TO REPORT ABOUT THE BATTLE OF MARATHON. THE POOR GUY DROPPED DEAD AT THE FINISH LINE, BUT THE LENGTH OF HIS RUN IS THE LENGTH OF TODAY'S RACE.

Asia

sia is a **HUGE** continent. It covers more area than North America, Europe, and Australia combined. It spans 90 degrees of latitude—from the Arctic Circle to the equator—and 150 degrees of longitude. Not only is Asia the biggest continent in area, it also has the biggest population. About half the world's population lives in Asia.

Asia has every type of landform and every type of climate. The highest mountains in the world—the **Himalayas**—are in Asia. Deserts cover much of the southwestern and central parts. Unlike many deserts, China's Gobi Desert is cold instead of hot, because it sits on a high plateau. Rainforests grow in much of southeastern Asia. The third largest river in the world, the **Yangtze River**, travels through China.

Russia is the largest country in Asia (even though some people say it's part of Europe). The smallest countries are islands—the Maldives and Bahrain. Many Asian countries are islands, and Indonesia is the largest group of islands in the world.

Even though Asia is so large, much of the land is mountains and deserts. So what do people do? They crowd into the cities by the coast or along a river. China has the biggest population of any country in the world, and India comes in a close second. Asia has many different cultures and many different kinds of people, plus it is the birthplace of five major religions: Christianity, Islam, Judaism, Buddhism, and Hinduism.

Largest Lake: *Caspian Sea (Russia)*

Lowest Point: *Dead Sea (Israel/Jordan)*

I rode I sailed I walked I sailed some more...

MARCO POLO'S LONG TRIP

Have you ever taken a really long trip? How about one that lasted twenty-four years? Marco Polo left his home in Italy when he was just a teenager, in 1271 (his dad came, too) and was one of the first Europeans to travel across Asia. It took him two dozen years to get back home! Europeans had always loved Asian silks and spices, but they were nearly impossible to get because there was no mapped-out route across Asia's 4,000 miles (6,400 km) of rough mountains and burning deserts. Marco Polo started his journey by sailing from Venice, Italy, to the Middle East. Then he walked south through Persia (now called Iran) and across the Gobi Desert to Beijing, China. This route was called the Silk Road. Polo later sailed along the coast of Asia to India and Sri Lanka. He took a northern route home, crossing the Black Sea. When he got back, he told stories of the incredible things he saw—and then everyone wanted to visit Asia!

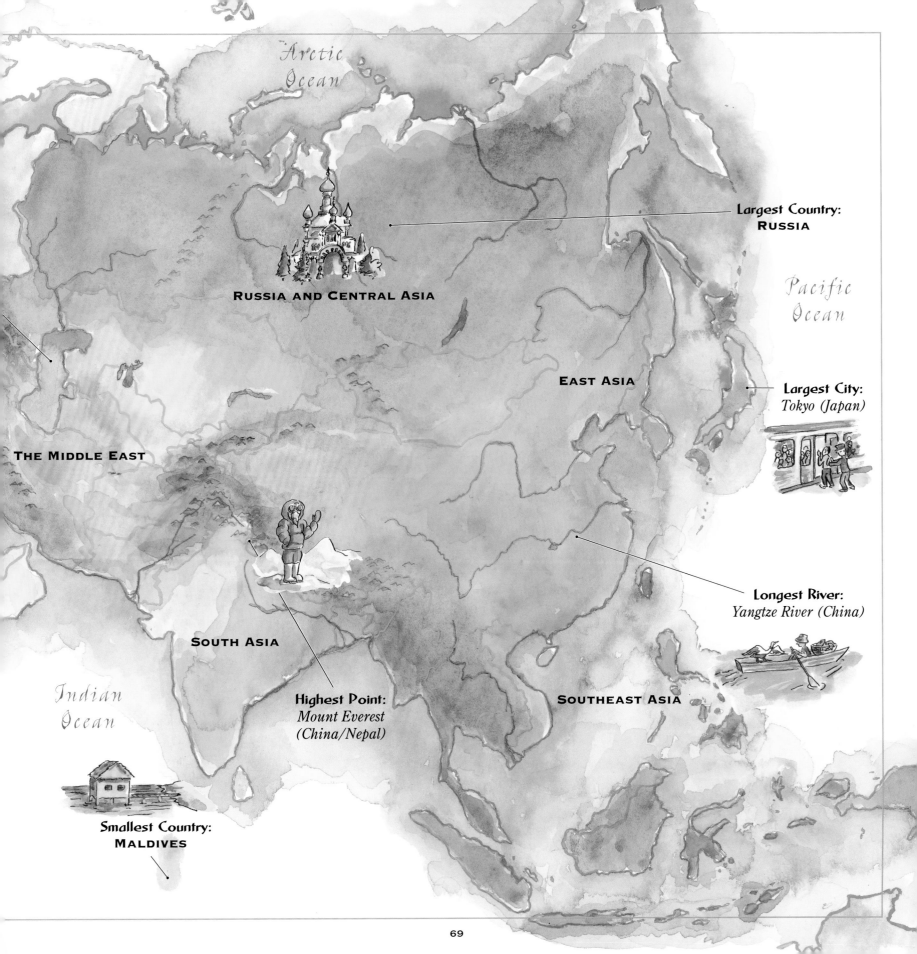

Arctic Ocean

Largest Country:
RUSSIA

RUSSIA AND CENTRAL ASIA

Pacific Ocean

EAST ASIA

Largest City:
Tokyo (Japan)

THE MIDDLE EAST

Longest River:
Yangtze River (China)

SOUTH ASIA

Indian Ocean

SOUTHEAST ASIA

Highest Point:
*Mount Everest
(China/Nepal)*

Smallest Country:
MALDIVES

Russia and Central Asia

The **Russian Federation**, called Russia, is the largest country in the world. It stretches across the entire northern part of Asia. Russia is so big that it has eleven time zones. The cities of Moscow and Saint Petersburg, in the western part of Russia, have long been centers of theater, art, and dance, with many famous dance and theater companies and museums.

The Russian land to the east of the Ural Mountains all the way to the Pacific Ocean is called **Siberia**. Siberia is thousands of miles of frozen tundra and thick taiga. Few people want to live there because it is bitterly cold (parts of Siberia are colder than the North Pole). The average winter temperature is -50°F (-46°C).

The countries of Central Asia are known for their grassy, flat, treeless **steppe**. Central Asia is also home to two enormous deserts—the Kyzyl Kum (Red Sand) and the Kara Kum (Black Sand). Many people in Central Asia are **nomads**, groups of people who have no permanent home but instead move from place to place. They are herders, and their animals—goats, sheep, and camels—provide them with milk and meat. When the animals eat all the grass in one area, it's time for the nomads to pack up their tents and move on.

In Russia, children each bring their teachers a bouquet of flowers on the first day of school.

MOSCOW IS THE CAPITAL OF RUSSIA.

SAINT PETERSBURG, RUSSIA, IS A CITY OF CANALS.

THE **ARAL SEA** BETWEEN UZBEKISTAN AND KAZAKHSTAN IS A FRESHWATER LAKE THAT OVER THE LAST FIFTY YEARS HAS SHRUNK IN HALF BECAUSE IT HAS BEEN OVERUSED FOR WATERING CROPS.

UZBEKISTAN WAS A KEY SPOT ON THE SILK ROAD.

KAZAKHSTAN
Astana

Caspian Sea

UZBEKISTAN
Ashgabat
TURKMENISTAN
Tashkent
Bishkek
KYRGYZSTAN
Dushanbe
AFGHANISTAN
TAJIKISTAN

Moscow

What You Need to Know about Russia and Central Asia

MAIN CROPS: WHEAT, TOBACCO, POTATOES, HAZELNUTS, SUNFLOWERS

MAIN LANGUAGES: RUSSIAN, KAZAKH, UZBEK, TAJIK, PASHTO, TURKMEN

CULTURAL HOLIDAYS: NEW YEAR, INTERNATIONAL WOMEN'S DAY, PROTECTOR OF THE MOTHERLAND DAY, VICTORY DAY, MELON DAY

SOME NATIVE ANIMALS: SIBERIAN TIGER, WEASELS, ARCTIC FOX

FAVORITE SPORTS: HOCKEY, SOCCER, TENNIS, BASKETBALL

FAVORITE FOODS: BORSCHT, CAVIAR, PIROSHKI, LAMB KEBAB, SHAWARMA, PILAF

INVENTIONS: HELICOPTER

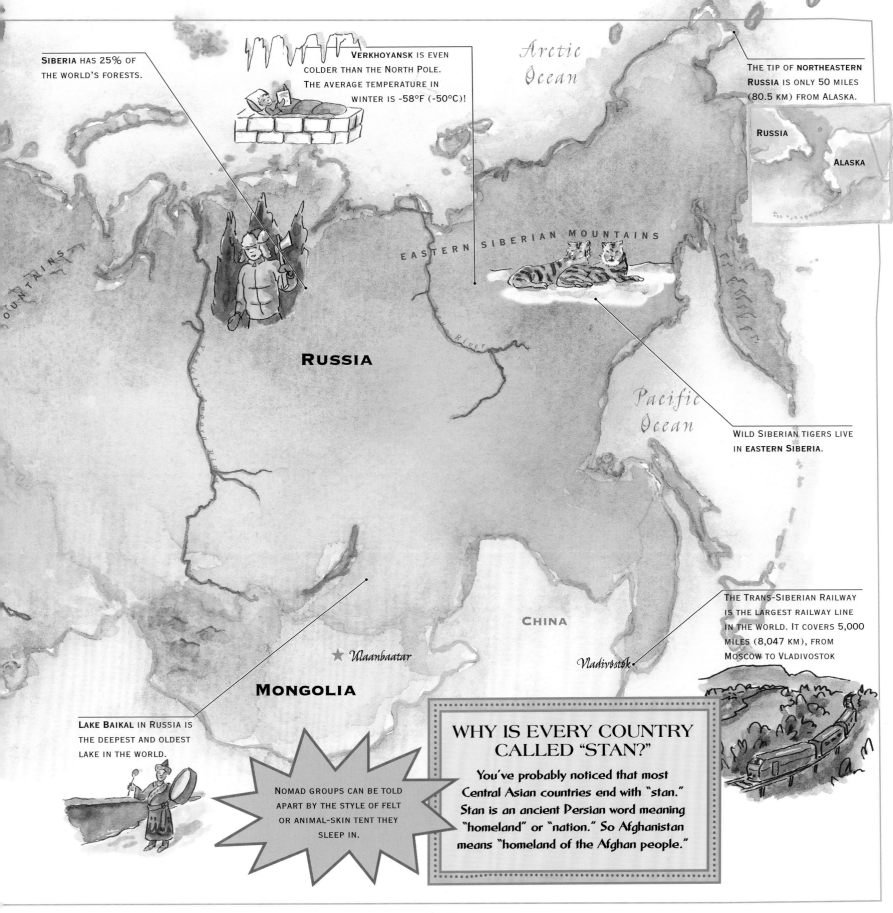

SIBERIA HAS 25% OF THE WORLD'S FORESTS.

VERKHOYANSK IS EVEN COLDER THAN THE NORTH POLE. THE AVERAGE TEMPERATURE IN WINTER IS -58°F (-50°C)!

Arctic Ocean

THE TIP OF NORTHEASTERN RUSSIA IS ONLY 50 MILES (80.5 KM) FROM ALASKA.

RUSSIA

ALASKA

EASTERN SIBERIAN MOUNTAINS

River

RUSSIA

Pacific Ocean

WILD SIBERIAN TIGERS LIVE IN EASTERN SIBERIA.

CHINA

★ *Ulaanbaatar*

MONGOLIA

Vladivostok

THE TRANS-SIBERIAN RAILWAY IS THE LARGEST RAILWAY LINE IN THE WORLD. IT COVERS 5,000 MILES (8,047 KM), FROM MOSCOW TO VLADIVOSTOK

LAKE BAIKAL IN RUSSIA IS THE DEEPEST AND OLDEST LAKE IN THE WORLD.

NOMAD GROUPS CAN BE TOLD APART BY THE STYLE OF FELT OR ANIMAL-SKIN TENT THEY SLEEP IN.

WHY IS EVERY COUNTRY CALLED "STAN?"

You've probably noticed that most Central Asian countries end with "stan." Stan is an ancient Persian word meaning "homeland" or "nation." So Afghanistan means "homeland of the Afghan people."

The Middle East

The lands surrounding the Mediterranean Sea and the Persian Gulf are called the **Middle East**. The name was created by the ancient Greeks, because from where they stood, this area was the Middle East, and India and China were the Far East. The Middle East is about deserts, oil, religion, ancient peoples, modern cities, and sandstorms.

More than half the **Arabian Peninsula** (Saudi Arabia, Yemen, Oman, United Arab Emirates, Qatar, and Kuwait) is desert. **Rub' al-Khali** (also called the Empty Quarter) is the largest sand desert in the world. The **An Nafūd** desert in Saudi Arabia is famous for its enormous sand dunes. **Bedouin**, nomads who live in the deserts, have been wandering this area with their herds of camels or goats for centuries. Freshwater is hard to find in the Middle East, so many countries are experimenting with desalination—taking the salt out of seawater.

The Middle East is rich in oil. About 65% of the world's oil comes from this area. Oil wells are dug deep into the ground and the oil is sucked out. The largest amount of oil has been found under the Arabian Desert. Oil has made the Middle East very wealthy. With the money from oil, they have built some modern, glittering cities.

The Middle East is an ancient land. **Mesopotamia**, one of the oldest known civilizations on the banks of the Tigris-Euphrates rivers, is now Iraq. Ancient Persia is now Iran. The Middle East is also the birthplace of three major religions: Christianity, Islam, and Judaism. Despite all the wealth and history, there has been constant fighting throughout the region for years—about where borders should be, about how to practice a religion, about how to govern, and about oil and freshwater.

LEBANON IS THE ONLY COUNTRY IN THE MIDDLE EAST THAT DOESN'T HAVE A DESERT.

JERUSALEM, ISRAEL, IS THE HOLY CITY FOR JUDAISM, CHRISTIANITY, AND ISLAM.

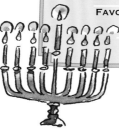

In Saudi Arabia, girls must wear veils in public. Some veils just cover the face, but others cover the entire body.

What You Need to Know about the Middle East

MAIN CROPS: OLIVES, PISTACHIOS, DATES, LIMES, POMEGRANATES

SOME NATIVE ANIMALS: ANGORA CAT, CAMEL, ARABIAN HORSE, ONYX

MAIN LANGUAGES: ARABIC, FARSI, HEBREW, KURDISH

CULTURAL HOLIDAYS: ÇOCUK BAYRAMI (CHILDREN'S DAY), HANUKKAH, PASSOVER, ROSH HASHANAH, RAMADAN, NOW RUZ

FAVORITE SPORTS: SOCCER, MOTOR SPORTS, CAMEL RACING

FAVORITE FOODS: HUMMUS, SHISH KEBAB, EGGPLANT, BAKLAVA, KIBBE

INVENTIONS: PERFUME, CARPETS

WHAT'S SO GREAT ABOUT OIL?

When it's cold in the winter, isn't it nice to turn on heat in your home? When you want to go to Disneyworld, isn't it better to drive in a car or fly in a plane than walk all the way there? Fuel for cars, airplanes, boats, and to heat your home or school comes from oil. The sticky, black resource gives over half the things on Earth power—and that's why people are willing to hand over a lot of money for it. But oil is a one-time deal. It's a nonrenewable resource, which means once we drain all the oil from our planet, the Earth will not produce any more.

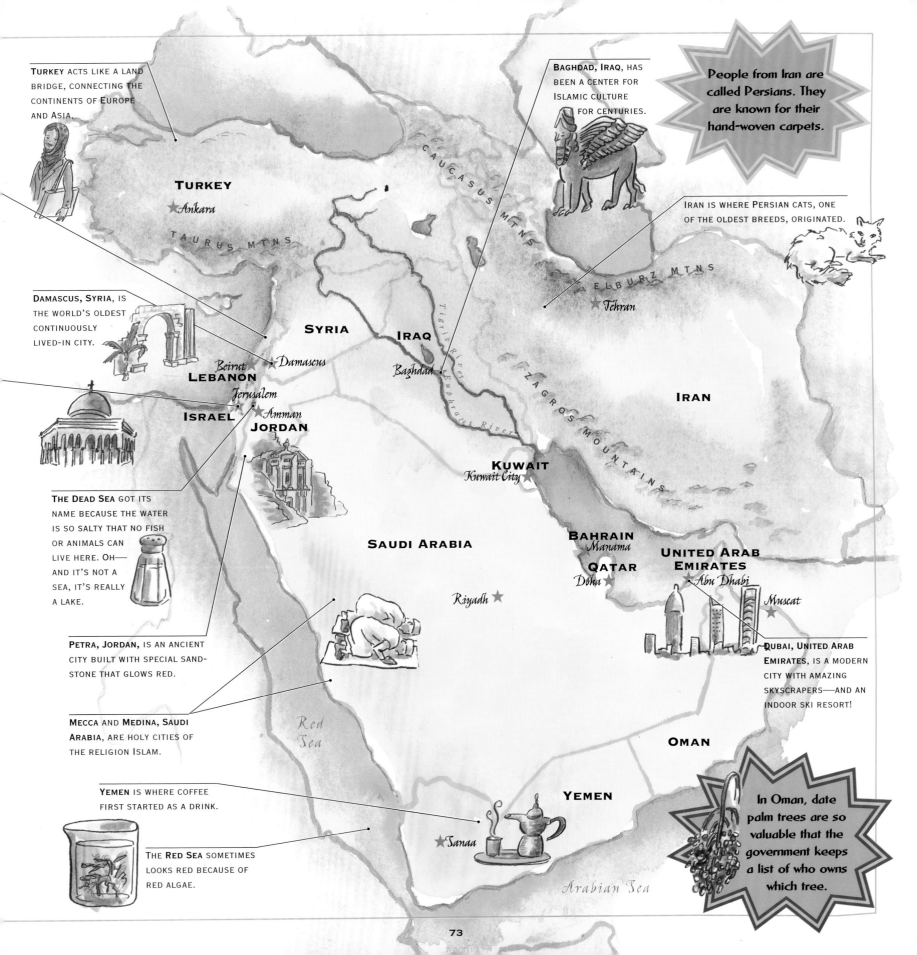

TURKEY ACTS LIKE A LAND BRIDGE, CONNECTING THE CONTINENTS OF EUROPE AND ASIA.

BAGHDAD, IRAQ, HAS BEEN A CENTER FOR ISLAMIC CULTURE FOR CENTURIES.

People from Iran are called Persians. They are known for their hand-woven carpets.

IRAN IS WHERE PERSIAN CATS, ONE OF THE OLDEST BREEDS, ORIGINATED.

DAMASCUS, SYRIA, IS THE WORLD'S OLDEST CONTINUOUSLY LIVED-IN CITY.

THE DEAD SEA GOT ITS NAME BECAUSE THE WATER IS SO SALTY THAT NO FISH OR ANIMALS CAN LIVE HERE. OH— AND IT'S NOT A SEA, IT'S REALLY A LAKE.

PETRA, JORDAN, IS AN ANCIENT CITY BUILT WITH SPECIAL SAND-STONE THAT GLOWS RED.

MECCA AND MEDINA, SAUDI ARABIA, ARE HOLY CITIES OF THE RELIGION ISLAM.

YEMEN IS WHERE COFFEE FIRST STARTED AS A DRINK.

THE RED SEA SOMETIMES LOOKS RED BECAUSE OF RED ALGAE.

DUBAI, UNITED ARAB EMIRATES, IS A MODERN CITY WITH AMAZING SKYSCRAPERS—AND AN INDOOR SKI RESORT!

In Oman, date palm trees are so valuable that the government keeps a list of who owns which tree.

TURKEY
Ankara
TAURUS MTNS
CAUCASUS MTNS
ELBURZ MTNS
Tehran
SYRIA
IRAQ
Damascus
Beirut
LEBANON
Jerusalem
Amman
ISRAEL
JORDAN
Baghdad
Tigris River
Euphrates River
ZAGROS MOUNTAINS
IRAN
KUWAIT
Kuwait City
SAUDI ARABIA
BAHRAIN
Manama
QATAR
Doha
UNITED ARAB EMIRATES
Abu Dhabi
Muscat
Riyadh
Red Sea
OMAN
YEMEN
Sanaa
Arabian Sea

73

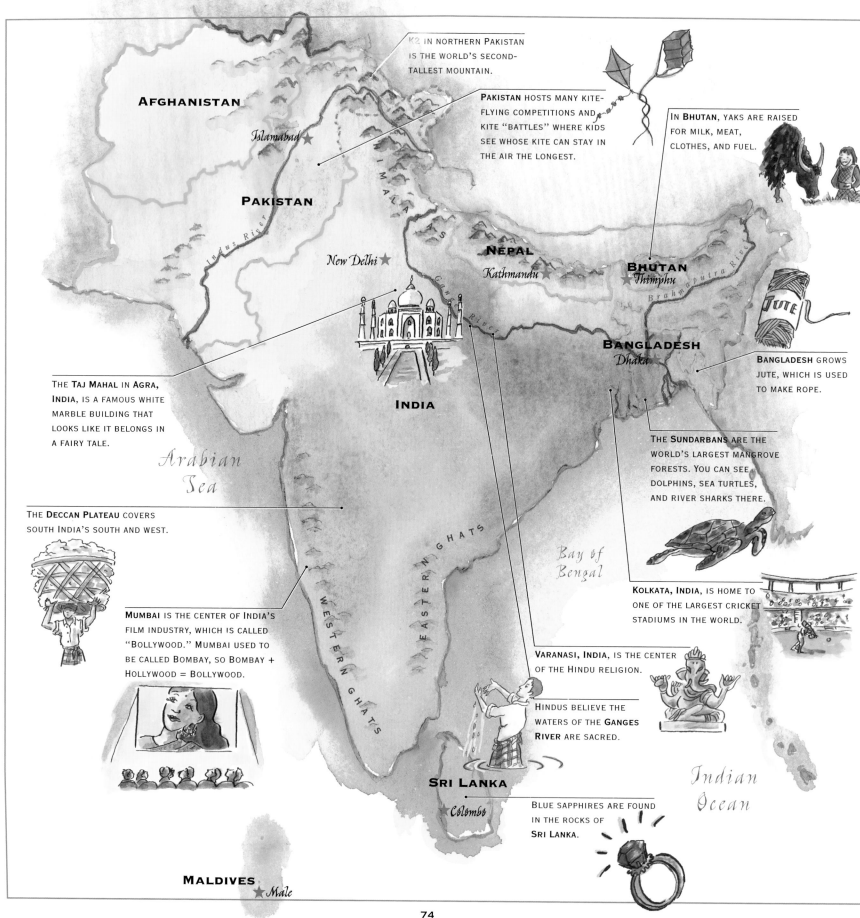

K2 IN NORTHERN PAKISTAN IS THE WORLD'S SECOND-TALLEST MOUNTAIN.

PAKISTAN HOSTS MANY KITE-FLYING COMPETITIONS AND KITE "BATTLES" WHERE KIDS SEE WHOSE KITE CAN STAY IN THE AIR THE LONGEST.

IN **BHUTAN**, YAKS ARE RAISED FOR MILK, MEAT, CLOTHES, AND FUEL.

AFGHANISTAN

Islamabad ★

PAKISTAN

Indus River

New Delhi ★

NEPAL

Kathmandu

BHUTAN
Thimphu

Brahmaputra River

BANGLADESH
Dhaka

BANGLADESH GROWS JUTE, WHICH IS USED TO MAKE ROPE.

Ganges River

INDIA

THE **TAJ MAHAL** IN **AGRA, INDIA**, IS A FAMOUS WHITE MARBLE BUILDING THAT LOOKS LIKE IT BELONGS IN A FAIRY TALE.

Arabian Sea

THE **SUNDARBANS** ARE THE WORLD'S LARGEST MANGROVE FORESTS. YOU CAN SEE DOLPHINS, SEA TURTLES, AND RIVER SHARKS THERE.

THE **DECCAN PLATEAU** COVERS SOUTH INDIA'S SOUTH AND WEST.

WESTERN GHATS

EASTERN GHATS

Bay of Bengal

MUMBAI IS THE CENTER OF INDIA'S FILM INDUSTRY, WHICH IS CALLED "BOLLYWOOD." MUMBAI USED TO BE CALLED BOMBAY, SO BOMBAY + HOLLYWOOD = BOLLYWOOD.

KOLKATA, INDIA, IS HOME TO ONE OF THE LARGEST CRICKET STADIUMS IN THE WORLD.

VARANASI, INDIA, IS THE CENTER OF THE HINDU RELIGION.

HINDUS BELIEVE THE WATERS OF THE **GANGES RIVER** ARE SACRED.

SRI LANKA

Colombo

BLUE SAPPHIRES ARE FOUND IN THE ROCKS OF **SRI LANKA**.

Indian Ocean

MALDIVES
★ *Male*

74

South Asia

The world's ten highest mountains are all found in South Asia. They are part of the Himalayas and other nearby ranges. The giant mountains are covered with snow, and as the snow melts it runs into the Ganges River that flows into India. The three great rivers of India—the Ganges, the Brahmaputra, and the Indus—all begin high up in the Himalayas.

India is the largest country in South Asia, with the second-largest population in the world. It is a land of opposites—it has extreme poverty yet also one of the fastest growing economies. Elephants roam its tribal areas yet its computer software is developed in high-rise office buildings. Its women and men wear traditional saris and dhotis, or designer European clothing. It is the birthplace of four religions (Hinduism, Buddhism, Jainism, and Sikhism), as well as the largest democracy in the world.

India is on a peninsula, surrounded by the Arabian Sea and the Bay of Bengal. Pakistan lies to its west. The countries of Bhutan and Nepal are nestled on the slopes of the Himalayas to its east. The tropical island nation of Sri Lanka is right off the coast of India in the Indian Ocean.

What You Need to Know about South Asia

MAIN CROPS: RICE, PINEAPPLE, MANGO, COTTON, SUGARCANE, JUTE

SOME NATIVE ANIMALS: TIGER, ELEPHANT, MONKEY, JACKAL, HYENA, PEACOCK

MAIN LANGUAGES: HINDI, ENGLISH, URDU, BENGALI, NEPALI, SINHALA

CULTURAL HOLIDAYS: DIWALI, ESALA PERAHERA, HOLI, RAKSHA BANDHAN, BASANT, PONGAL, SHIVA RATRI

FAVORITE SPORTS: CRICKET, FIELD HOCKEY, SQUASH

FAVORITE FOODS: MASALA, TANDOORI, CHAPATI, CHAI

INVENTIONS: CHESS, PAJAMAS, BADMINTON, SHAMPOO, YOGA

CRICKET IS A SPORT THAT DATES BACK EIGHT CENTURIES. IT'S SIMILAR TO BASEBALL BUT IS PLAYED WITH A FLAT BAT, AND THE PLAYERS RUN BACK AND FORTH INSTEAD OF AROUND THE FIELD.

Holiday Highlight

BROTHERS AND SISTERS IN INDIA CELEBRATE A HOLIDAY EVERY AUGUST CALLED **RAKSHA BANDHAN**. DURING A SPECIAL CEREMONY, GIRLS TIE A SILK BRACELET AROUND THEIR BROTHER'S WRIST, AND THE BOYS PROMISE TO PROTECT THEIR SISTERS. THE SIBLINGS GIVE EACH OTHER CANDY AND GIFTS.

The Sherpa people of Nepal are famous mountaineers. When a climber tries to reach the summit of Mount Everest, he or she will take along a Sherpa guide.

The Name Game

MANY CITY NAMES IN INDIA HAVE CHANGED RECENTLY. THE OLD NAMES WERE GIVEN BY THE BRITISH MANY YEARS AGO, WHEN THEY CONTROLLED INDIA. THE NEW NAMES COME FROM INDIAN CULTURE AND THEIR MAIN LANGUAGE, HINDI.

OLD NAME	NEW NAME
BOMBAY	MUMBAI
CALCUTTA	KOLKATA
MADRAS	CHENNAI
PONDICHERRY	PUDUCHERRY

Southeast Asia

Southeast Asia is all about water . . . and islands. Although there is a mainland area, much of Southeast Asia is bordered by water. Southeast Asia is made up of two peninsulas and thousands of islands. Indonesia is the largest archipelago in the world—about 13,500 islands. The Philippines has 7,100 islands. That's a lot of islands! If you live in Southeast Asia, you definitely need a boat!

Southeast Asia is very mountainous, with big areas of hot, humid rainforest. Most mountains in Southeast Asia are covered with thick forest and jungle. Some areas are very rural, such as the country of Myanmar, and some are very urban, such as Singapore and Thailand.

Most people in mainland Southeast Asia live along the valleys by a river. This is one of the biggest rice-growing areas of the world, especially by the Mekong Delta in Vietnam. Farmers grow their rice in **paddies** (fields flooded with water), which are on hillsides, and they are **terraced** (this means they look like stairs). Terracing keeps the water from running down the hill and washing away all the rice.

A **monsoon** is heavy rain with wind that blows in from the ocean. Farmers rely on monsoons for growing rice. **Typhoons** (the Pacific Ocean version of the hurricane) pound the Southeast Asian islands every year, flooding the land and destroying homes.

What You Need to Know about Southeast Asia

MAIN CROPS: RICE, PINEAPPLES, RUBBER, TEAK, COCONUTS
SOME NATIVE ANIMALS: ELEPHANT, ORANGUTAN, KOMODO DRAGON, GIBBON
MAIN LANGUAGES: THAI, BURMESE, VIETNAMESE, KHMER, MALAY, FILIPINO, BAHASA INDONESIAN
CULTURAL HOLIDAYS: TRUNG THU, SONGKRAN
FAVORITE SPORTS: KICK VOLLEYBALL
FAVORITE FOODS: SPRING ROLLS, GADO-GADO, SATAY
INVENTIONS: PC SOUND CARD

Don't touch someone's head in **Indonesia** or you'll bring on bad luck. Indonesians believe that a person's soul is in his or her head and is easily hurt if touched.

RANGOON, MYANMAR, HAS A GLITTERY-GOLD BUDDHIST TEMPLE, CALLED A **PAGODA**, TOWERING ABOVE THE CITY STREETS.

BANGKOK, THAILAND, IS A HUGE CITY WITH OVER 6 MILLION PEOPLE. THERE ARE SO MANY CARS AND SO FEW ROADS THAT THERE IS ALWAYS A TRAFFIC JAM.

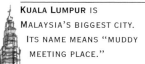

KUALA LUMPUR IS MALAYSIA'S BIGGEST CITY. ITS NAME MEANS "MUDDY MEETING PLACE."

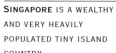

SINGAPORE IS A WEALTHY AND VERY HEAVILY POPULATED TINY ISLAND COUNTRY.

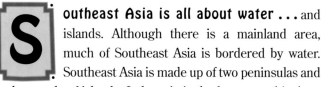

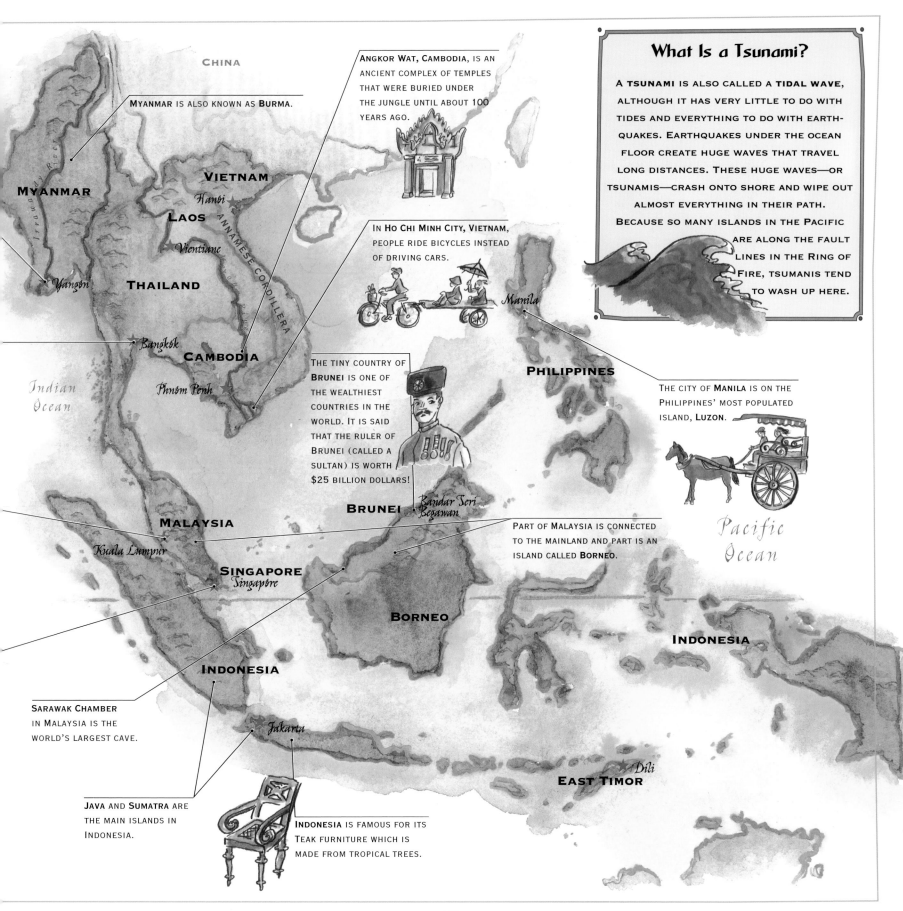

CHINA

MYANMAR IS ALSO KNOWN AS BURMA.

ANGKOR WAT, CAMBODIA, IS AN ANCIENT COMPLEX OF TEMPLES THAT WERE BURIED UNDER THE JUNGLE UNTIL ABOUT 100 YEARS AGO.

What Is a Tsunami?

A TSUNAMI IS ALSO CALLED A TIDAL WAVE, ALTHOUGH IT HAS VERY LITTLE TO DO WITH TIDES AND EVERYTHING TO DO WITH EARTH-QUAKES. EARTHQUAKES UNDER THE OCEAN FLOOR CREATE HUGE WAVES THAT TRAVEL LONG DISTANCES. THESE HUGE WAVES—OR TSUNAMIS—CRASH ONTO SHORE AND WIPE OUT ALMOST EVERYTHING IN THEIR PATH. BECAUSE SO MANY ISLANDS IN THE PACIFIC ARE ALONG THE FAULT LINES IN THE RING OF FIRE, TSUMANIS TEND TO WASH UP HERE.

MYANMAR

VIETNAM

Irrawaddy River

Hanoi

LAOS

Vientiane

ANNAMESE CORDILLERA

Yangon

THAILAND

IN HO CHI MINH CITY, VIETNAM, PEOPLE RIDE BICYCLES INSTEAD OF DRIVING CARS.

Manila

Bangkok

CAMBODIA

Indian Ocean

Phnom Penh

THE TINY COUNTRY OF BRUNEI IS ONE OF THE WEALTHIEST COUNTRIES IN THE WORLD. IT IS SAID THAT THE RULER OF BRUNEI (CALLED A SULTAN) IS WORTH $25 BILLION DOLLARS!

PHILIPPINES

THE CITY OF MANILA IS ON THE PHILIPPINES' MOST POPULATED ISLAND, LUZON.

BRUNEI

Bandar Seri Begawan

MALAYSIA

Kuala Lumpur

PART OF MALAYSIA IS CONNECTED TO THE MAINLAND AND PART IS AN ISLAND CALLED BORNEO.

Pacific Ocean

SINGAPORE

Singapore

BORNEO

INDONESIA

INDONESIA

SARAWAK CHAMBER IN MALAYSIA IS THE WORLD'S LARGEST CAVE.

Jakarta

Dili

EAST TIMOR

JAVA AND SUMATRA ARE THE MAIN ISLANDS IN INDONESIA.

INDONESIA IS FAMOUS FOR ITS TEAK FURNITURE WHICH IS MADE FROM TROPICAL TREES.

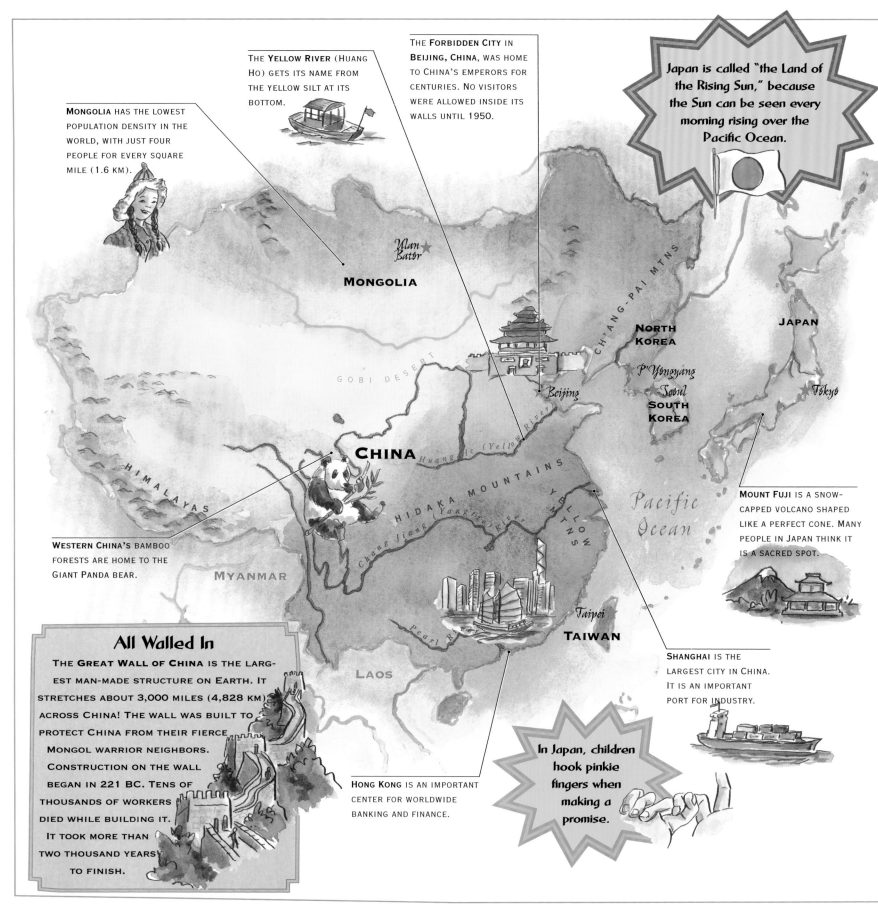

THE YELLOW RIVER (HUANG HO) GETS ITS NAME FROM THE YELLOW SILT AT ITS BOTTOM.

THE FORBIDDEN CITY IN BEIJING, CHINA, WAS HOME TO CHINA'S EMPERORS FOR CENTURIES. NO VISITORS WERE ALLOWED INSIDE ITS WALLS UNTIL 1950.

Japan is called "the Land of the Rising Sun," because the Sun can be seen every morning rising over the Pacific Ocean.

MONGOLIA HAS THE LOWEST POPULATION DENSITY IN THE WORLD, WITH JUST FOUR PEOPLE FOR EVERY SQUARE MILE (1.6 KM).

Ulan Bator ★

MONGOLIA

GOBI DESERT

CH'ANG-PAI MTNS

NORTH KOREA

JAPAN

Beijing

P'Yongyang

Seoul

SOUTH KOREA

Tōkyō

CHINA

Huang He (Yellow River)

HIDAKA MOUNTAINS

YELLOW MTNS

Pacific Ocean

H I M A L A Y A S

Chang Jiang (Yangtze) River

MOUNT FUJI IS A SNOW-CAPPED VOLCANO SHAPED LIKE A PERFECT CONE. MANY PEOPLE IN JAPAN THINK IT IS A SACRED SPOT.

WESTERN CHINA'S BAMBOO FORESTS ARE HOME TO THE GIANT PANDA BEAR.

MYANMAR

Taipei

TAIWAN

Pearl R.

SHANGHAI IS THE LARGEST CITY IN CHINA. IT IS AN IMPORTANT PORT FOR INDUSTRY.

All Walled In

THE GREAT WALL OF CHINA IS THE LARGEST MAN-MADE STRUCTURE ON EARTH. IT STRETCHES ABOUT 3,000 MILES (4,828 KM) ACROSS CHINA! THE WALL WAS BUILT TO PROTECT CHINA FROM THEIR FIERCE MONGOL WARRIOR NEIGHBORS. CONSTRUCTION ON THE WALL BEGAN IN 221 BC. TENS OF THOUSANDS OF WORKERS DIED WHILE BUILDING IT. IT TOOK MORE THAN TWO THOUSAND YEARS TO FINISH.

LAOS

HONG KONG IS AN IMPORTANT CENTER FOR WORLDWIDE BANKING AND FINANCE.

In Japan, children hook pinkie fingers when making a promise.

East Asia

East Asia is hugely taken up by China. China is the fourth largest country in size, and it has the largest population in the world. One out of every five people on Earth lives in China! Most of them live in the plains of eastern China. China is also the most bordered country in the world—fourteen different countries touch it. China has one of the oldest civilizations, and for thousands of years it was way ahead of Europe in science and inventing.

Jutting out from China is the Korean Peninsula. Korea is divided into two very different countries. South Korea is a modern, wealthy country. It has low plains and river valleys that are good for growing rice. North Korea is very poor. It is very cold and mountainous so few crops can grow well.

Japan is a mountainous string of more than three thousand islands in the Pacific Ocean. Most of the population lives on the four main islands of Hokkaido, Honshu, Kyushu, and Shikoku. Even though it has very few natural resources, Japan has managed to build itself into a world power by making computers and electronics. Japan is on the Pacific Ring of Fire where three tectonic plates collide, giving the islands many typhoons, earthquakes, and tsunamis.

WHAT IS AN EARTHQUAKE?

The word "quake" means "to shake," so an "earthquake" is when the earth rocks and rolls right under your feet! Earthquakes only last a minute or two, but they can topple buildings and trees. An earthquake happens when the tectonic plates under the Earth's surface bump into one another or slide under one another. This force causes the earth surface to crack a little, called a **fault line**. When the plates along the fault line rub against one another, it causes the shaking.

The Chinese languages are made up of several thousand characters. English is made up of only twenty-six!

Holiday Highlight

THE **CHINESE NEW YEAR** IS A HUGE, FIFTEEN-DAY CELEBRATION. PEOPLE WEAR RED CLOTHING, GIVE CHILDREN MONEY IN RED ENVELOPES, AND WATCH FIREWORKS AND PARADES FEATURING HUGE SILK-AND-PAPER DRAGONS. DRAGONS ARE VERY POPULAR ANIMALS IN CHINESE STORIES.

What You Need to Know about East Asia

MAIN CROPS: RICE, BAMBOO, WHEAT, TEA

MAIN LANGUAGES: MANDARIN CHINESE, JAPANESE, KOREAN

CULTURAL HOLIDAYS: CHINESE NEW YEAR, OBON, SOLNAL (KOREAN NEW YEAR), TANABATA, CHING MING FESTIVAL

SOME NATIVE ANIMALS: GIANT PANDA, WILD YAK, TIGER, SNOW LEOPARD, CRANE

FAVORITE SPORTS: TABLE TENNIS, VOLLEYBALL, ARCHERY, WRESTLING, MARTIAL ARTS

FAVORITE FOODS: SUSHI, RICE, DUMPLINGS, KIMCHI, GREEN AND BLACK TEA

INVENTIONS: ICE CREAM, GUNPOWDER, SILK, RAZOR SCOOTER, CALLIGRAPHY

Africa is a world record-winning continent:

- Africa has fifty-three countries—the **most countries** of any continent.
- Africa is home to the Sahara Desert, the **largest desert** in the world. The Sahara runs from the Atlantic Ocean to the Red Sea.
- Africa is home to the Nile River, the **longest river** in the world. The Nile flows from south to north, from Uganda to Egypt.
- Africa is the only continent with land in all four hemispheres.

Africa is the second-largest continent and comes very close to being an island. It is surrounded by the Atlantic Ocean, the Indian Ocean, the Mediterranean Sea, and the Red Sea, and it is ttached to Asia only by the tiny Sinai Peninsula in Egypt. Yet oddly enough, Africa has the shortest coast of all the continents, because it has so few bays and peninsulas. The equator slices through the middle of Africa, dividing it into sections: the northern part is desert, the southern part is **savanna**, a flat area covered by grass, and the area by the equator is rainforest.

All humans come from Africa—no matter where you, or your grandparents, or your grandparents' grandparents were born. Scientists have found skeletons to prove that all our ancestors started out millions of years ago in the area by Tanzania and Ethiopia. Today, the people of Africa belong to thousands of ethnic groups, or **tribes**. Each tribe has its own language. There are over one thousand different languages spoken here. African people often speak three or four languages fluently.

Africa has a lot of different people, and it also has a lot of different animals. No other continent has as many wild animals. Have you ever heard of an African safari? That's when people from all over the world travel to Africa to take an up-close look at the animals—lions, cheetahs, gazelles, zebras, rhinoceros, elephants, and so many more. But human traffic combined with hunting has turned Africa into the continent with the most endangered animals. Protecting the wildlife, before it all disappears, is now a matter of life or death.

I was discovered FIRST!

How much older?

But I'm OLDER!

1.2 million years! And, I even walked upright

Thats not FAIR...

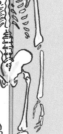

Really Old Relatives

IN THE AFAR DESERT OF ETHIOPIA, SCIENTISTS HAVE FOUND PIECES OF FOSSIL SKELETONS OF WHAT THEY BELIEVE TO BE THE ANCESTORS OF THE FIRST HUMANS. THE PRE-HUMAN FOSSILS DATE BACK ABOUT FOUR MILLION YEARS AGO. SCIENTISTS NAMED THE SKELETONS "LUCY" AND "ARDI." THESE FOSSILS ARE IMPORTANT FOR SCIENTISTS STUDYING HUMAN EVOLUTION, TO HELP THEM BETTER UNDERSTAND HOW HUMANS CHANGED AND DEVELOPED OVER TIME.

Lucy *Ardi*

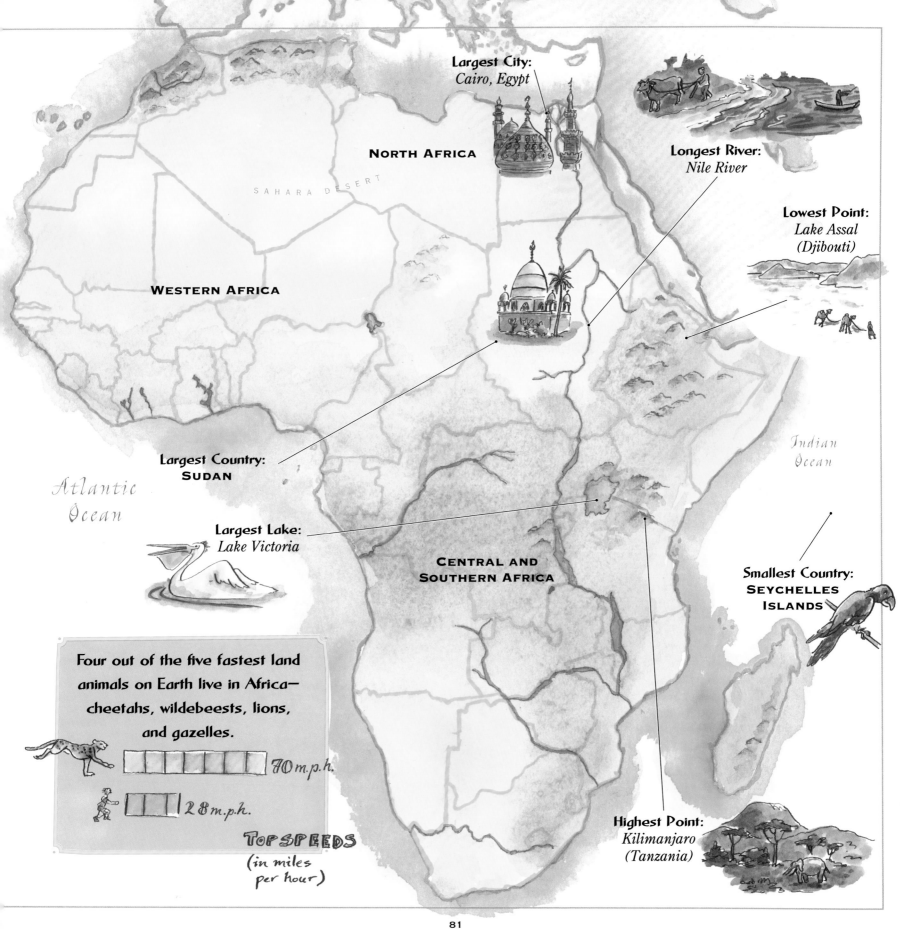

Largest City:
Cairo, Egypt

NORTH AFRICA

SAHARA DESERT

Longest River:
Nile River

Lowest Point:
*Lake Assal
(Djibouti)*

WESTERN AFRICA

*Atlantic
Ocean*

Largest Country:
SUDAN

Largest Lake:
Lake Victoria

*Indian
Ocean*

**CENTRAL AND
SOUTHERN AFRICA**

**Smallest Country:
SEYCHELLES
ISLANDS**

Four out of the five fastest land
animals on Earth live in Africa—
cheetahs, wildebeests, lions,
and gazelles.

70 m.p.h.

28 m.p.h.

TOP SPEEDS
(in miles
per hour)

Highest Point:
*Kilimanjaro
(Tanzania)*

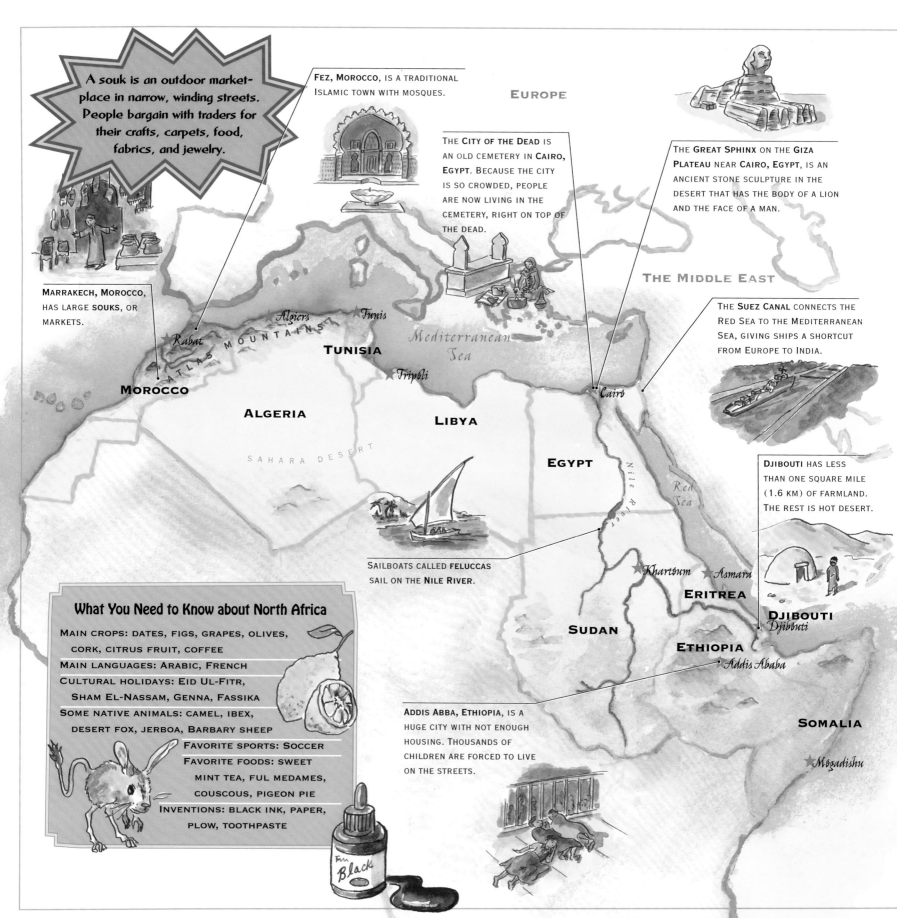

A souk is an outdoor market-place in narrow, winding streets. People bargain with traders for their crafts, carpets, food, fabrics, and jewelry.

FEZ, MOROCCO, IS A TRADITIONAL ISLAMIC TOWN WITH MOSQUES.

THE CITY OF THE DEAD IS AN OLD CEMETERY IN CAIRO, EGYPT. BECAUSE THE CITY IS SO CROWDED, PEOPLE ARE NOW LIVING IN THE CEMETERY, RIGHT ON TOP OF THE DEAD.

EUROPE

THE GREAT SPHINX ON THE GIZA PLATEAU NEAR CAIRO, EGYPT, IS AN ANCIENT STONE SCULPTURE IN THE DESERT THAT HAS THE BODY OF A LION AND THE FACE OF A MAN.

MARRAKECH, MOROCCO, HAS LARGE SOUKS, OR MARKETS.

THE MIDDLE EAST

THE SUEZ CANAL CONNECTS THE RED SEA TO THE MEDITERRANEAN SEA, GIVING SHIPS A SHORTCUT FROM EUROPE TO INDIA.

Algiers   Tunis

Mediterranean Sea

Rabat

ATLAS MOUNTAINS

TUNISIA

Tripoli

MOROCCO

ALGERIA

LIBYA

EGYPT

Cairo

SAHARA DESERT

Nile River

Red Sea

DJIBOUTI HAS LESS THAN ONE SQUARE MILE (1.6 KM) OF FARMLAND. THE REST IS HOT DESERT.

SAILBOATS CALLED FELUCCAS SAIL ON THE NILE RIVER.

Khartoum   Asmara

ERITREA

DJIBOUTI
Djibouti

What You Need to Know about North Africa

MAIN CROPS: DATES, FIGS, GRAPES, OLIVES, CORK, CITRUS FRUIT, COFFEE

MAIN LANGUAGES: ARABIC, FRENCH

CULTURAL HOLIDAYS: EID UL-FITR, SHAM EL-NASSAM, GENNA, FASSIKA

SOME NATIVE ANIMALS: CAMEL, IBEX, DESERT FOX, JERBOA, BARBARY SHEEP

FAVORITE SPORTS: SOCCER

FAVORITE FOODS: SWEET MINT TEA, FUL MEDAMES, COUSCOUS, PIGEON PIE

INVENTIONS: BLACK INK, PAPER, PLOW, TOOTHPASTE

SUDAN

ETHIOPIA
Addis Ababa

SOMALIA

ADDIS ABBA, ETHIOPIA, IS A HUGE CITY WITH NOT ENOUGH HOUSING. THOUSANDS OF CHILDREN ARE FORCED TO LIVE ON THE STREETS.

Mogadishu

Black

North Africa

North Africa is dominated by the huge Sahara Desert, which is the size of the entire United States. The Sahara is not a sandy desert, it is actually covered with rock and gravel. During the day, the temperature is scorching hot, but at night, it drops to freezing cold. The Sahara gets less than 10 in (25 cm) of rain a year, but **oasis** towns are found in Libya and Egypt. An oasis is a place in the desert where underground water rises up.

For hundreds of years, the Sahara cut off Northern Africa from the rest of the continent (it was too much of a pain to try to cross the huge hot gravel pit!), so the ancient people traded with the people from Asia. As a result, North Africa speaks mostly Arabic, and the culture is very Arab-influenced. The countries of Egypt, Libya, and Tunisia are often grouped with the Middle East. Egypt is one of the oldest civilizations. Ancient pyramids built as tombs for the pharaohs still stand in the desert and attract many tourists. The biggest pyramid contains 2 million blocks that each weigh 2.5 tons!

The eastern part of Africa (Ethiopia, Eritrea, Djibouti, and Somalia) is called the **Horn of Africa**, because it looks like the horn of a rhinoceros poking out into the Indian Ocean. Most people who live here are bedouin. The area is very dry because of **drought**, a long period of time with no rain. Without enough rain, crops and animals die, and people sometimes starve because there is no food.

THE WORD *SAHARA* IN ARABIC MEANS "DESERT." SO THE SAHARA DESERT IS REALLY THE "DESERT DESERT."

WATER . . . PLEASE!

Can you imagine walking for eight hours to get a glass of water? That's what many kids in Africa are forced to do. One of Africa's biggest problems is water. There is none—or almost none. Only half the people can get fresh drinking water, and often they have to walk for miles and miles to find it. And when they finally do find it, the water is often contaminated and it makes them sick. Water-related diseases are the number one cause of death in Africa. Many organizations around the world are working to get clean water to this continent.

Western Africa

THE WATERS OFF MAURITANIA ATTRACT FISHING FLEETS FROM ALL OVER THE WORLD.

WHAT IS COLONIALISM?

A colony is a foreign land that is ruled by a larger country without permission—and that's exactly what happened to Africa. In the 1800s, the major European countries (Great Britain, France, Portugal, Spain, Belgium, Germany, Holland, and Italy) came over to Africa and saw all the riches it had to offer. Everyone in Europe wanted diamonds, gold, ivory, and a mug of good coffee. Each European country claimed a piece of the land, drawing borders on a map that had absolutely nothing to do with people and tribes that had been in Africa for centuries. Some tribes were divided into different countries. The Europeans gave their colonies European-sounding names. It wasn't until the 1950s and '60s that the African countries regained their independence and renamed themselves.

1914

☐ Italy
☐ Portugal
☐ Spain

☐ Belgium
☐ France
☐ Germany
☐ Great Britain
☐ Independent

Western Africa is like a cafeteria line of climates and biomes. It starts off with desert in the north and then moves onto the **sahel**, dry grasslands on the edge of the desert. A bit farther down the line to the south is savanna and then, at the end, tropical rainforest. West Africa is on the "bulge of Africa," because the land bulges out into the Atlantic Ocean.

West Africa is a very rural area, with many cocoa, palm oil, coffee, and peanut farms. Timber used to be a big industry, but many trees have been cut down, leaving very little forest. There are hundreds of different tribes living in West Africa, and in the last few decades, there have been a lot of bloody civil wars, with different groups of people within a country fighting for power. War has created much poverty and made many children unable to go to school.

Atlantic Ocean

PEANUTS GROW UNDERGROUND, AND IN AFRICA, THEY ARE CALLED GROUNDNUTS.

DAKAR, SENEGAL, IS THE WESTERNMOST POINT OF AFRICA.

What You Need to Know about West Africa

MAIN CROPS: COFFEE, COCOA, RUBBER, COTTON, YAMS
SOME NATIVE ANIMALS: CROCODILE, MONKEY, MANATEE, MEERKAT, HIPPOPOTAMUS
MAIN LANGUAGES: ARABIC, FRENCH, ENGLISH
CULTURAL HOLIDAYS: ABOAKYERE, INDEPENDENCE DAY, EID UL-FITR, CHILDREN'S DAY, EID UL-KABIR, NEW YAM FESTIVAL
FAVORITE SPORTS: SOCCER
FAVORITE FOODS: CASSAVA, PEANUT STEW, JOLLOF RICE, KENKEY
INVENTIONS: WORLD'S FASTEST COMPUTER

GUINEA IS RICH WITH BAUXITE, A MINERAL USED TO MAKE ALUMINUM.

West Africa used to be called the Gold and Ivory Coast because of all the gold and ivory (from elephant tusks) traded there.

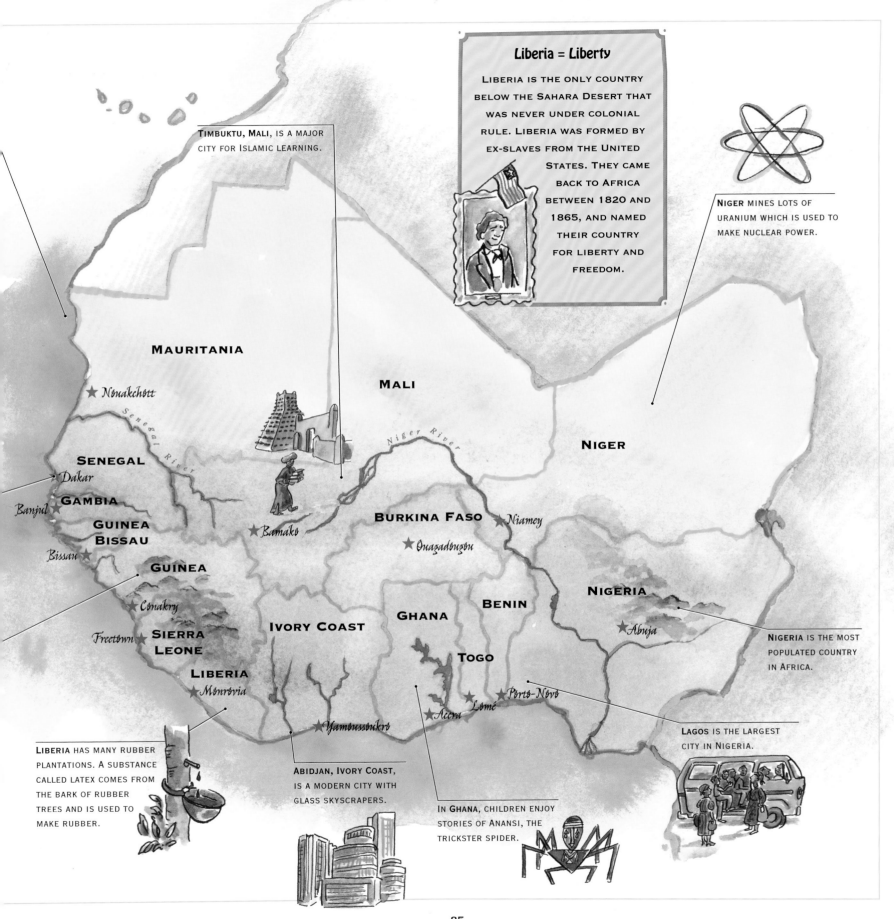

TIMBUKTU, MALI, IS A MAJOR CITY FOR ISLAMIC LEARNING.

Liberia = Liberty

LIBERIA IS THE ONLY COUNTRY BELOW THE SAHARA DESERT THAT WAS NEVER UNDER COLONIAL RULE. LIBERIA WAS FORMED BY EX-SLAVES FROM THE UNITED STATES. THEY CAME BACK TO AFRICA BETWEEN 1820 AND 1865, AND NAMED THEIR COUNTRY FOR LIBERTY AND FREEDOM.

NIGER MINES LOTS OF URANIUM WHICH IS USED TO MAKE NUCLEAR POWER.

MAURITANIA

★ Nouakchott

Senegal River

MALI

Niger River

NIGER

SENEGAL

★ Dakar

GAMBIA

Banjul

GUINEA BISSAU

Bissau

GUINEA

★ Conakry

Freetown

SIERRA LEONE

LIBERIA

★ Monrovia

★ Bamako

BURKINA FASO

★ Niamey

★ Ouagadougou

IVORY COAST

GHANA

BENIN

NIGERIA

★ Abuja

TOGO

★ Pôrto-Nôvo

★ Accra ★ Lomé

★ Yamoussoukro

NIGERIA IS THE MOST POPULATED COUNTRY IN AFRICA.

LAGOS IS THE LARGEST CITY IN NIGERIA.

LIBERIA HAS MANY RUBBER PLANTATIONS. A SUBSTANCE CALLED LATEX COMES FROM THE BARK OF RUBBER TREES AND IS USED TO MAKE RUBBER.

ABIDJAN, IVORY COAST, IS A MODERN CITY WITH GLASS SKYSCRAPERS.

IN GHANA, CHILDREN ENJOY STORIES OF ANANSI, THE TRICKSTER SPIDER.

Central and Southern Africa

The land south of the Sahara desert is called **sub-Saharan** ("sub" means "under" or "below"). The **Great Rift Valley** covers the east coast of Africa from Ethiopia to Mozambique. It is a huge crack in the Earth that was formed millions of years ago when two tectonic plates under the surface pulled apart. The Great Rift is a series of deep valleys with wide savannas and huge lakes. **Mount Kilimanjaro**, the highest mountain in Africa, is in the Great Rift Valley. The yellow-grass plains contain the most amazing animals. Big areas of the savanna have been turned into protected game parks, such as the Serengeti in Tanzania and the Masai Mara in Kenya.

The southernmost part of Africa has two large deserts—the **Kalahari** and the **Namib**. The Kalahari is home to the San, one of the last tribes of hunter-gatherers in the world. The Namib Desert, which means "place of nothingness," has giant red sand dunes. Most of central and southern Africa is rural. People live in villages, herd livestock, and grow only enough food for their family. Botswana and Zimbabwe, on the southern tip, are the wealthiest countries because of their diamond and gold mines.

Madagascar

MADAGASCAR IS A ONE-OF-A-KIND ISLAND OFF THE COAST OF SOUTH AFRICA. MADAGASCAR IS HOME TO ANIMALS AND PLANTS THAT ARE NOT FOUND ANYWHERE ELSE IN THE WORLD, SUCH AS THE LEMUR AND SPECIAL KINDS OF ORCHIDS. HALF OF THE WORLD'S VANILLA (A VERY IMPORTANT PART OF VANILLA ICE CREAM!) IS ALSO HARVESTED ON THIS ISLAND.

What You Need to Know about Central and South Africa

MAIN CROPS: PEANUTS, TEA, COFFEE, CASSAVA, YAMS, COCONUTS

SOME NATIVE ANIMALS: OSTRICH, LION, GIRAFFE, CHEETAH

MAJOR LANGUAGES: KISWAHILI (SWAHILI), FRENCH, ENGLISH, PORTUGUESE, AFRIKAANS

CULTURAL HOLIDAYS: N'CWALA, KENYATTA DAY, HEROES' DAY, WORKERS' DAY, INTERNATIONAL WOMEN'S DAY

FAVORITE SPORTS: SOCCER, CRICKET, RUGBY

FAVORITE FOODS: NYAMA CHOMA, BOEREWORS, CORN PORRIDGE

INVENTIONS: SWIMMING POOL VACUUM, HEART TRANSPLANT, CAT SCAN

IN 2007, A 7,000 CARAT DIAMOND WAS FOUND IN SOUTH AFRICA!

POACHING INTO EXTINCTION

Poaching—the illegal killing of wild animals—is a major problem in Africa. The central and southern African forests and savannas used to be filled with huge wild animals. Then in the 1970s and '80s, gangs of poachers came in and hunted elephants for their ivory tusks, lions and cheetahs for their hides, rhinos for their horns, and gorillas to use their hands and heads as trophies. In the 1980s, more than eight hundred thousand elephants were killed, and the rhino population decreased by 83%. The gorilla population is half of what it once was—only about seven hundred silverback mountain gorillas remain in the wild. Scientists predict that if poaching continues many African animals will be extinct in fifteen years! Can you imagine an Africa with no elephants, no lions, and no gorillas? It is up to all of us to stop the poachers, by not buying ivory, exotic meats, and hides.

NOTICE: This preserve is PATROLLED

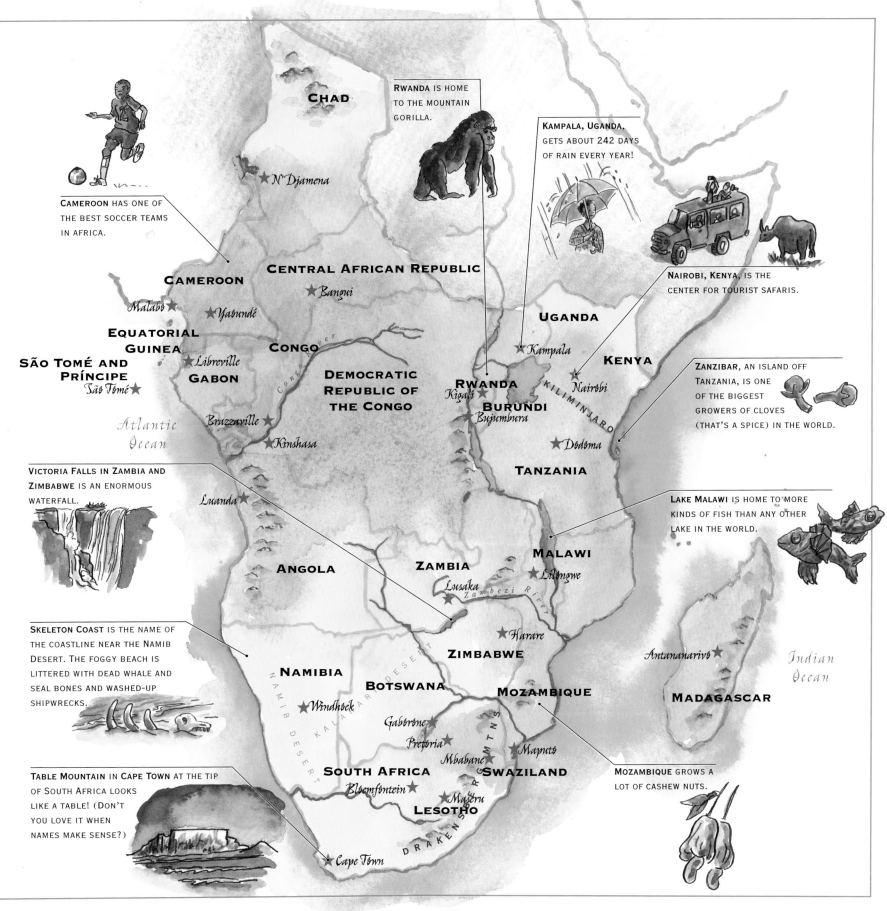

CAMEROON HAS ONE OF THE BEST SOCCER TEAMS IN AFRICA.

RWANDA IS HOME TO THE MOUNTAIN GORILLA.

KAMPALA, UGANDA, GETS ABOUT 242 DAYS OF RAIN EVERY YEAR!

NAIROBI, KENYA, IS THE CENTER FOR TOURIST SAFARIS.

ZANZIBAR, AN ISLAND OFF TANZANIA, IS ONE OF THE BIGGEST GROWERS OF CLOVES (THAT'S A SPICE) IN THE WORLD.

VICTORIA FALLS IN ZAMBIA AND ZIMBABWE IS AN ENORMOUS WATERFALL.

LAKE MALAWI IS HOME TO MORE KINDS OF FISH THAN ANY OTHER LAKE IN THE WORLD.

SKELETON COAST IS THE NAME OF THE COASTLINE NEAR THE NAMIB DESERT. THE FOGGY BEACH IS LITTERED WITH DEAD WHALE AND SEAL BONES AND WASHED-UP SHIPWRECKS.

TABLE MOUNTAIN IN CAPE TOWN AT THE TIP OF SOUTH AFRICA LOOKS LIKE A TABLE! (DON'T YOU LOVE IT WHEN NAMES MAKE SENSE?)

MOZAMBIQUE GROWS A LOT OF CASHEW NUTS.

CHAD
N'Djamena

CENTRAL AFRICAN REPUBLIC
Bangui

CAMEROON
Malabo
Yaoundé

EQUATORIAL GUINEA

SÃO TOMÉ AND PRÍNCIPE
São Tomé

CONGO
Libreville

GABON

DEMOCRATIC REPUBLIC OF THE CONGO

Brazzaville
Kinshasa

UGANDA
Kampala

KENYA
Nairobi

RWANDA
Kigali

BURUNDI
Bujumbura

KILIMINJARO

TANZANIA
Dodoma

Atlantic Ocean

Luanda

ANGOLA

ZAMBIA
Lusaka
Zambezi River

MALAWI
Lilongwe

Harare

ZIMBABWE

NAMIB DESERT

KALAHARI DESERT

NAMIBIA
Windhoek

BOTSWANA
Gaborone

MOZAMBIQUE
Maputo

Antananarivo

MADAGASCAR

Indian Ocean

SOUTH AFRICA
Pretoria
Mbabane
SWAZILAND
Bloemfontein
Maseru
LESOTHO

DRAKENSBERG MTNS

Cape Town

Australia

t's island time!

Australia is an island surrounded by the Indian Ocean and the Pacific Ocean. It's the largest island in the world, but the smallest continent—and the only continent that is just one country. Its nickname is **"the Land Down Under"** because it's located completely in the Southern Hemisphere, far below the equator.

Oceania is the name given to about twenty-five thousand small volcanic islands in the South Pacific. New Zealand and Papua New Guinea are the largest of these islands.

Back to Australia . . .

Australia is the flattest and driest country in the world. It is divided into six states: New South Wales, Queensland, South Australia, Tasmania, Victoria, and Western Australia. The **Aborigines** were the original settlers, about forty-five thousand years ago. The Dutch were the first European explorers to reach Australia, approaching it from the west. They found only dry flatland along the west, north, and south coasts, so they went back home without ever checking out the continent's mountainous and wet east coast. But the British explored farther. In 1827, they named the land Australia from a Latin word that means "southern." For years, the British shipped their prisoners (and anyone else they didn't like) there. Australia was like a huge floating jail.

The **Great Dividing Range** is a long mountain range on the east coast of Australia. It divides the eastern lowlands from the central highlands. Most of the rain in Australia falls here, making the land good for farming and

Continent Record Holders

Highest point
Mount Kosciuszko

Lowest Point
Lake Eyre

Longest river
Murray River

Largest Lake
Lake Eyre

Largest city
Sydney

GREAT BARRIER REEF

The Great Barrier Reef, off the northern coast of Australia, is the longest coral reef in the world—1,300 miles (2,100 km) long. It is the largest structure built by a living organism—and that includes humans. It's even bigger than the tallest skyscrapers. And it's the only living structure visible from outer space!

The Great Barrier Reef is home to about one-third of all marine life—four thousand species of fish, seven hundred species of coral, and thousands of plant and life. Coral reefs are often called the "rainforest of the ocean," because of the variety of living species is greater than almost anywhere in the world.

Most people think coral is a kind of plant. Wrong! Coral is an animal, called a coral polyp. A coral polyp has a soft body, stomach, and tentacles—kind of like a jellyfish. Coral polyps use the minerals in seawater to build a limestone skeleton around themselves. Polyps live close together with very little personal space, kind of like kids in a school hallway between classes. As the polyps grow, they build new skeletons on top of the old ones. As millions of skeletons pile up, a reef is formed. Coral reefs are built very, very, very slowly.

Mouth

Stomach

Skeleton

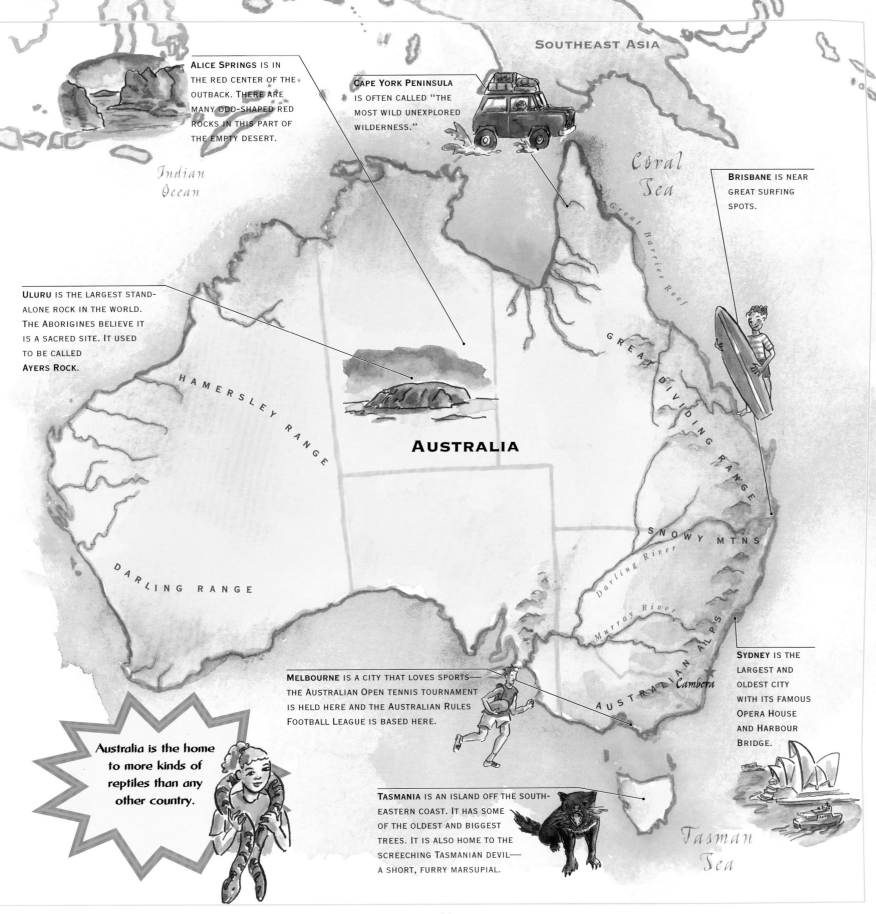

ALICE SPRINGS IS IN THE RED CENTER OF THE OUTBACK. THERE ARE MANY ODD-SHAPED RED ROCKS IN THIS PART OF THE EMPTY DESERT.

CAPE YORK PENINSULA IS OFTEN CALLED "THE MOST WILD UNEXPLORED WILDERNESS."

BRISBANE IS NEAR GREAT SURFING SPOTS.

ULURU IS THE LARGEST STAND-ALONE ROCK IN THE WORLD. THE ABORIGINES BELIEVE IT IS A SACRED SITE. IT USED TO BE CALLED AYERS ROCK.

SOUTHEAST ASIA

Indian Ocean

Coral Sea

Great Barrier Reef

HAMERSLEY RANGE

AUSTRALIA

DARLING RANGE

GREAT DIVIDING RANGE

SNOWY MTNS

Darling River

Murray River

AUSTRALIAN ALPS

Canberra

SYDNEY IS THE LARGEST AND OLDEST CITY WITH ITS FAMOUS OPERA HOUSE AND HARBOUR BRIDGE.

MELBOURNE IS A CITY THAT LOVES SPORTS—THE AUSTRALIAN OPEN TENNIS TOURNAMENT IS HELD HERE AND THE AUSTRALIAN RULES FOOTBALL LEAGUE IS BASED HERE.

Australia is the home to more kinds of reptiles than any other country.

TASMANIA IS AN ISLAND OFF THE SOUTH-EASTERN COAST. IT HAS SOME OF THE OLDEST AND BIGGEST TREES. IT IS ALSO HOME TO THE SCREECHING TASMANIAN DEVIL—A SHORT, FURRY MARSUPIAL.

Tasman Sea

89

raising sheep. Australia raises more sheep than any other country does (and makes the most wool sweaters). Most people live near the Great Dividing Range, and almost all the major cities are here. The hot and dry plains of the Great Artesian Basin are west of the Great Dividing Range. Animals can survive here, because there is **artesian water**, which is water that comes up to the surface from underground.

One-third of Australia—from the center to the west coast—is dry, sand-and-rock desert. It is called "the Outback," because it is *out in the back* of the mountains and rivers. Few people live here. The strong winds have eroded a lot of the red-colored desert rocks, carving them into pillars or domes called **buttes**.

What You Need to Know about Australia

MAIN CROPS: EUCALYPTUS, KIWI, WHEAT

MAIN LANGUAGE: ENGLISH (BUT THERE ARE OVER 250 ABORIGINAL LANGUAGES)

CULTURAL HOLIDAYS: AUSTRALIA DAY, ANZAC DAY, QUEEN'S BIRTHDAY, BOXING DAY

SOME NATIVE ANIMALS: KANGAROO, KOALA, WOMBAT, EMU, PLATYPUS

FAVORITE SPORTS: SURFING, RUGBY, TENNIS, CRICKET, AUSTRALIAN RULES FOOTBALL

FAVORITE FOODS: PAVLOVA, MEAT PIE, VEGEMITE, ANZAC BISCUITS

INVENTIONS: BOOMERANG, BUNGEE JUMPING, CAR RADIO, ELECTRIC DRILL, BIONIC EAR

HUGE SHEEP FARMS ARE CALLED **STATIONS** IN AUSTRALIA AND NEW ZEALAND.

JAMES COOK AND THE SOUTH SEAS

In the 1700s, the Europeans thought there was just one huge continent in the South Pacific—a giant "Southern Continent." They didn't know about all of the other islands. Captain James Cook of Great Britain cleared up the confusion. He made three voyages to the area from 1768 to 1779 and called dibs on Australia for Great Britain. He saw that Australia, New Zealand, and the Solomon Islands were separate countries and filled in the blanks of the world map. Cook and his crew were the first Europeans to see a kangaroo (They were very confused by it, and argued over what kind of animal it could be). Cook sailed close enough to Antarctica to realize it was another southern continent, but he had to turn back because of the "ice mountains," as he called the icebergs.

Oceania

Let's not forget Oceania . . .

New Zealand is made up of two large islands and a bunch of smaller islands, all off the southeast of Australia. South Island is mountainous and North Island is volcanic. In New Zealand, there are ten times more sheep than people.

The other islands of Oceania are separated into three groups: Melanesia; Micronesia; and Polynesia.

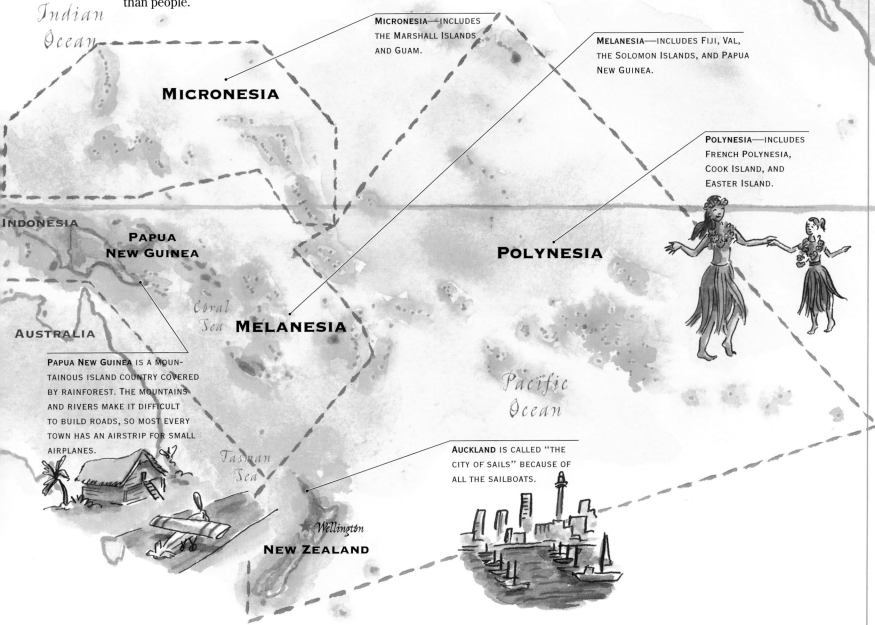

Indian Ocean

MICRONESIA—INCLUDES THE **MARSHALL ISLANDS** AND **GUAM**.

MELANESIA—INCLUDES **FIJI**, **VAL**, THE **SOLOMON ISLANDS**, AND **PAPUA NEW GUINEA**.

MICRONESIA

POLYNESIA—INCLUDES **FRENCH POLYNESIA**, **COOK ISLAND**, AND **EASTER ISLAND**.

INDONESIA

PAPUA NEW GUINEA

POLYNESIA

Coral Sea

MELANESIA

AUSTRALIA

PAPUA NEW GUINEA IS A MOUNTAINOUS ISLAND COUNTRY COVERED BY RAINFOREST. THE MOUNTAINS AND RIVERS MAKE IT DIFFICULT TO BUILD ROADS, SO MOST EVERY TOWN HAS AN AIRSTRIP FOR SMALL AIRPLANES.

Pacific Ocean

Tasman Sea

AUCKLAND IS CALLED "THE CITY OF SAILS" BECAUSE OF ALL THE SAILBOATS.

★ *Wellington*

NEW ZEALAND

Antarctica and the Arctic Regions

Antarctica is cold. We're talking fingertips-falling-off cold. Breath-freezing-in-less-than-a-second cold. We're talking an average winter day is -125°F (-87C°). It's also the iciest, windiest, and driest place on Earth. It's no big surprise that, even though Antarctica is the fifth-largest continent, no one lives there. There are no flowering plants, no grass, and no large mammals. Just ice. A lot of ice. Sheets of ice up to 3 miles (5 km) thick cover the continent. The ice sheets are more than 14 million years old. The ice is made of freshwater, and three-quarters of the world's freshwater is trapped in this ice.

Antarctica means "opposite the Arctic"—which it is. The center of Antarctica is the South Pole. Antarctica is considered a desert, because it never rains or snows. Because Antarctica is huge and frozen, it was the last continent to be explored. And if you think about it, Antarctica is the only continent to truly be discovered because no one lived there before the European explorers arrived.

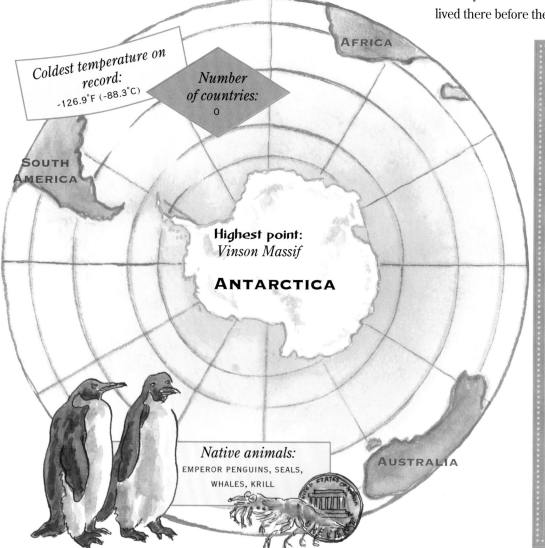

Coldest temperature on record:
-126.9°F (-88.3°C)

Number of countries:
0

Highest point:
Vinson Massif

ANTARCTICA

AFRICA

SOUTH AMERICA

AUSTRALIA

Native animals:
EMPEROR PENGUINS, SEALS,
WHALES, KRILL

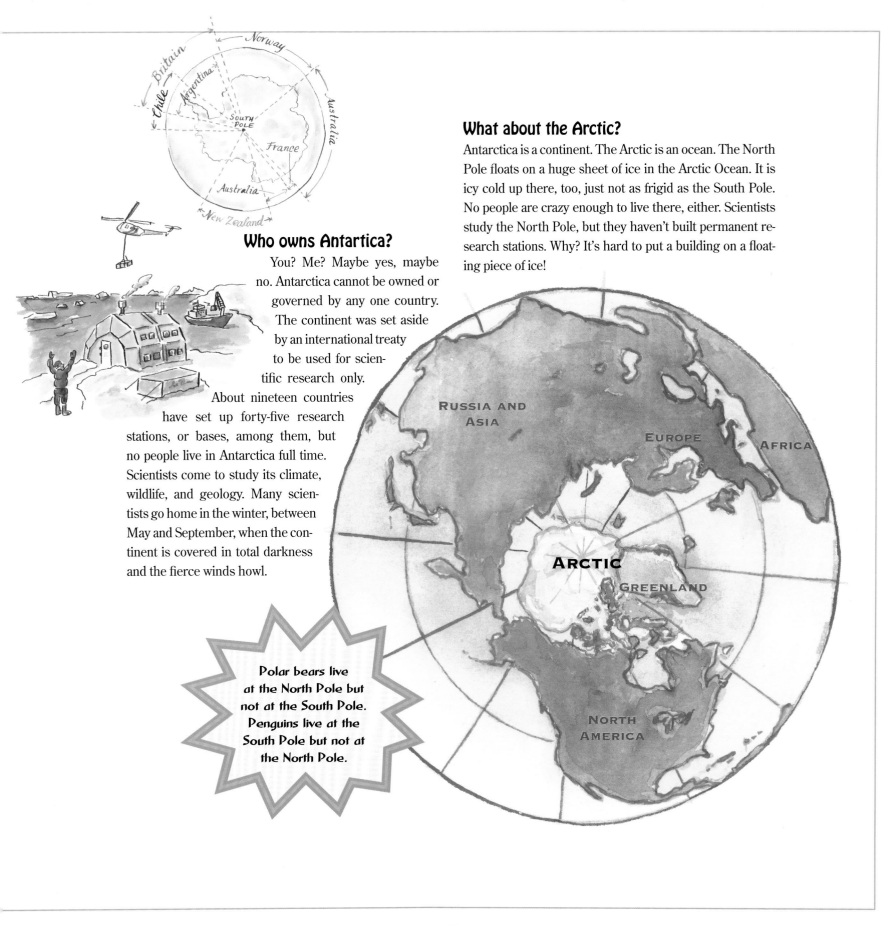

What about the Arctic?

Antarctica is a continent. The Arctic is an ocean. The North Pole floats on a huge sheet of ice in the Arctic Ocean. It is icy cold up there, too, just not as frigid as the South Pole. No people are crazy enough to live there, either. Scientists study the North Pole, but they haven't built permanent research stations. Why? It's hard to put a building on a floating piece of ice!

Who owns Antartica?

You? Me? Maybe yes, maybe no. Antarctica cannot be owned or governed by any one country. The continent was set aside by an international treaty to be used for scientific research only.

About nineteen countries have set up forty-five research stations, or bases, among them, but no people live in Antarctica full time. Scientists come to study its climate, wildlife, and geology. Many scientists go home in the winter, between May and September, when the continent is covered in total darkness and the fierce winds howl.

Polar bears live at the North Pole but not at the South Pole. Penguins live at the South Pole but not at the North Pole.

Index

More about Geography

Brainwaves. *The Most Fantastic Atlas of the Whole Wide World.* New York: Dorling Kindersley, 2008.

Gardner, Jane and J. Elizabeth Mills. *The Everything Kids Geography Book.* Massachusetts: Adams Media, 2009.

National Geographic Student Atlas of the World. Washington DC: National Geographic Society, 2009.

Rosenthal, Paul. *Where on Earth: A Geografunny Guide to the Globe.* New York: Alfred A. Knopf, Inc., 1992.

Tucci, Paul A. and Matthew T. Rosenberg. *The Handy Geography Answer Book.* Michigan: Visible Ink Press, 2009.

More about Experiments and Crafts

Rhatigan, Joe, and Heather Smith. *Geography Crafts for Kids.* New York: Lark Books, 2002.

Van Cleave, Janice. *Geography for Every Kid.* New York: John Wiley & Sons, 1993.

More about World Culture

Kindersley, Barnabas, and Anabel Kindersley. *Children Just Like Me.* New York: Dorling Kindersley Publishing Inc., 1995.

Milord, Susan. *Hands Around the World.* Vermont: Williamson Publishing, 1992.

Read about It on the Web

www.cia.gov/library/publications/the-world-factbook/

www.enchantedlearning.com/geography

www.firstschoolyears.com/geography

www.geography4kids.com

www.geography.about.com

www.kidsgeo.com

www.mbgnet.net

www.nationalgeographic.com

www.science.nasa.gov

www.socialstudiesforkids.com

www.worldalmanacforkids.com

Play Geography Games on the Web

www.eduplace.com/geonet/

www.fedstats.gov/kids/mapstats/

www.kids.nationalgeographic.com/games/geographygames

Are you a geography whiz? The National Geographic Bee is an annual geography contest for students in grades 4-8 in the United States. Ask your teacher about it.